*This book is dedicated to the memory of Alyssa,
may the butterfly always be a reminder of her beautiful
spirit that lives on in the garden of our hearts.*

INTRODUCTION

Some time ago I experienced an awakening, Father God took me on a journey of discovery, a journey of pondering His creation. I began reading Genesis 1, The Creation Story, the creation of our beautiful planet, and, in particular The Garden where He created the first Man and Woman, and all living creatures.

This was only to be the beginning, my love of creation has led me to living as we were once designed, in harmony with our world, eating only what was provided in The Garden and to provide a home for many of His creatures who no longer have a home.

What began as a desire to love Gods creation has grown into a passion for devoting my time by offering a sanctuary to those unwanted; a haven to little creatures, and in particular guinea pigs, who want to live out their days in peace, without need and fear as they had once done.

When the time comes for them to return to The Garden from where they first came, we send them off, with love and a prayer, we will cheer them on as they make their way back to the place where they were first imagined, by The Way of the Covenant and into the lush green of The Garden.

These are the stories of a guinea pig named Lowey, the first created being of the creatures that creep on the ground. Come on a journey with Lowey as he shares his life in The Garden, and discovers how to live in a new world when his world is shattered and The Garden is no longer his home.

In loving memory of Bear, Sherman, Indy and Daniel.

CHAPTER 1

In The Beginning

G enesis 1:1 In the beginning God created the heavens and the earth.

Waking, breathing, feeling, hearing, smelling and seeing, these are all unrecognisable until we have the experience of being born, but what about creation, being formed from the dust, being spoken into existence? Let there be! And it was good!

Lowey's eyes blinked open, the light from the sun dancing on the water caused him to shut them as quickly as they had opened. He could feel the warmth of the sun wrap around him like a blanket of peace, and yet the light breeze was ruffling his fur at the same time. Lowey wanted to move, but the warmth and the caress of the breeze enticed him to stay there and not move. His chest moved slowly up and down with his breath, and he could feel the hot air on his lips as it escaped on its way out. He opened his eyes once again, this time adjusting to the brightness, aware of the sound of water as it bubbled past him on its way to a distant place. The softness of the ground held him in its arms; he felt safe.

Lowey was filled with an understanding of who he was, where he was and why. He hadn't experienced these things; he just knew them, and he was here. He slowly lifted his paws and admired them; the claws were a glistening black, delicate and pointed, the digits were adorned with a beautiful ginger fur, soft and wavy. He was taken with the beauty of them and the way the hair moved with the breeze.

"I am fearfully and wonderfully made," he thought.

He was unable to hold back the smile that spread across his lips. He leapt to his feet and admired himself in the clear water of the stream.

Lowey announced to the Garden, "I am very well rounded; I couldn't have made myself any better! Well rounded, in the sense that everything is perfect, of course."

His coat was curly and matched his feet in colour and softness, there were many colours mixed, so many shades of brown and ginger, with just a sprinkling of black that accentuated his snowy white nose, but what stood out were the whiskers long and white, but with a slight curl in each one.

He brushed some pieces of grass from his tummy. "There! That's better," he said.

Lowey had become so engrossed by his reflection that he hadn't noticed that he was no longer alone. Off in the distance, he could hear voices, and he could hear the tall grass behind him begin to rustle. Filled with a sudden rush of excitement, Lowey turned and bounded forward, his curly little bottom wiggling from side to side as if with a life of its own.

"Hello?" Lowey called out, pushing his head into the thick mound of grass. He wriggled his bottom and moved a little further until his head was poking out the other side. Lowey peered around expecting to see someone, but all that came into view was a rocky outcrop surrounded by giant reeds gently swaying as if inviting Lowey to come closer. Edging closer and calling out again hoping to encourage a response, his nose began to twitch. He tilted his head and was transfixed by the sweet scent drifting on the breeze of the flowers and grasses, Lowey realised he could name them, he knew the names of all the flowers and trees!

"I am filled with all knowledge," he thought proudly. "I am the Knower of all things in this Garden." Suddenly Lowey remembered the others in the Garden that he was looking for and began to call out again.

"Hello, my name is Lowey, I am the Created Knower of all things in this Garden," he called out.

"If I am genuinely the Knower of all things in this Garden, then why do I not know who is hiding from me? Hmm?" Lowey thought that perhaps he should rephrase his bold statement, and clearing his throat, he stood up as tall as he could on his back legs and announced, "My name is Lowey, and I am The Created Knower of most things in the Garden, please come out and show yourself, I promise I will thrill you with my sheer beauty!"

Lowey stretched up as high as he could, checking his coat for anything that may have adhered itself, and picking off a couple of pieces of grass he regarded them in his paw and then flicked them through the air coming back down onto all fours.

"There you are!' A loud voice boomed with joy. 'Come here to me!"

Two giant hands wrapped around Lowey, holding him in a firm but not too tight grip and gently lifting him into the air. Lowey's heart was pounding as he was raised upwards. With his eyes closed tight he struggled with all his might to wriggle free, but to no avail. Lowey began to screech at the top of his lungs.

"Put me down, help me someone!"

Suddenly he had stopped moving upwards and now a hot breath blew into Lowey's face, tickling his whiskers. Opening one eye, he looked between the giant fingers.

"Oh, my, oh my!" Lowey screeched, and closed his eye again. "Maybe this is a dream, that's it, I'm asleep," but the breathing continued. Opening both eyes this time, he peered through the enormous fingers. The Man's face was huge and adorned with swirls of beautiful fur, not nearly as perfect as his own of course, but beautiful none the less, it glistened with gold and red, there was fur above his eyes and on the top of his head, but everywhere else was naked.

"He too is a magnificent creature," Lowey thought.

The Man smiled widely at Lowey and let out another huge laugh. Lowey closed his eyes a little, but then opened them bravely lifting his head to get a better view of the cavernous mouth.

"You are a cheeky one!" said the Man. "What am I going to call you?"

"Lowey!" Lowey replied, "You can call me Lowey," he said standing to his feet, and gingerly balancing on the massive hand, "I Am The Knower of most things in this Garden, and I am fearfully and wonderfully made!"

"All right, all right," said the Man "Just calm down. I only wanted to say hello and give you a name. You are squealing like a pig - I am going to call you a Cavy, but you are going to be known as a Guinea Pig or piggie!"

Lowey stood dumbfounded. He stuck a claw into his ear and gave it a jiggle around. Lowey found that the ear jiggling seemed to help him think, and suddenly he shrieked at the top of his lungs. "Why? Why, would he give me a new name?" Now he was standing up, taller than ever. "I don't know why you think you can give me a new name, the one I have is perfectly fine!"

"All right, all right" said the Man, "Down you go then," and before Lowey knew it, he was back in the long protective grass and bounding as fast as his little legs would take him towards the security of the rocks. The reeds were waving him on again, beckoning him to run faster.

"Run, Lowey," he thought and don't look back. He quickly ducked in behind the safety of the rocks. His breath coming faster from his mouth, and his chest pounding,

"Oh my, oh my, oh my," he cried. He had finally made it to safety, sitting with his head in his paws, he leaned back against the coolness of the rock.

"Oh, please do not let me be alone here with this giant," he wailed. Even though the giant had not hurt Lowey, he had given him a new name, and that did hurt. "A piggie? How ridiculous," snorted Lowey.

Sitting quietly for some time, Lowey realised that all the running had made his mouth parched; he needed to find something to drink. The stream, the stream where I woke up! Yes! Lowey jumped to his feet and forgetting all about the silly name that the Man had given him, he set off in the direction of the stream.

Pushing his way back through the tall grass, he noticed that it was very lush and plentiful. "Poaceoe!" Lowey muttered to himself; "I know the name of the grass! How tall and proud it also stands!"

Stepping out of the opening by the stream, he couldn't help but notice how the stream babbled away to itself, swirling around the stones and lovingly caressing the grassy banks. "This is truly a glorious place," he thought.

Now on all fours, Lowey trotted forward towards the edge of the grassy riverbank and immediately became aware of how thirsty he was for the cool water. He positioned his front feet in such a way that he could lean into the stream without slipping in. Finally, he drank deeply; the water was cold and fresh on his tongue, he could feel the little bubbles in his throat as he swallowed a mouthful, it was so satisfying he thought he might never stop.

Suddenly Lowey caught a glimpse of something out of the corner of his eye and stopped drinking mid gulp, turning his head slowly he swallowed. Sitting not too far away was another little creature with similar features, only smaller in stature. "Oh, what a magnificent sight," Lowey thought. Tiny beads of waters glistened on the ends of his whiskers, and he wiped his mouth with the back of his little ginger paw. The new arrival was now up and standing on all fours and sniffing the air, looking intently at Lowey.

"Hello!" Lowey said, "My name is Lowey and …" suddenly he was cut off mid-sentence as the new little creature snatched the conversation from him.

"I'm Savannah. I thought that I was alone here in The Garden, but now you are here, and I am so pleased." She spoke in such a hurried high-pitched voice Lowey found himself blinking in time with her words.

"I woke up and here I was, and I just knew everything. I am quite brilliant you know; I can tell you the names of all the plants and the trees, the grasses and flowers. Isn't it exciting?" Savannah shrieked at Lowey.

By this time, Lowey had his little hairy paws covering his ears, he couldn't believe somebody so small and cute could make such a noise.

"Oh, alright," said Lowey removing his paws from his ears and standing up on two legs. He placed one paw on what was his waist and wiggled his little claw on the other paw in her direction.

"I can see that you are very excited, but could you please just lower your voice a little?" A droplet of water slid down Lowey's whisker and fell onto the ground. Feeling a little rattled now as he was still thirsty, he tried not to show his irritation. He smiled at Savannah and placed his paw on hers.

"Come and join me for a drink and then we can sit and get to know each other, and you can tell me all about how you came to be here in the Garden."

Savannah moved closer to the embankment, now down on all fours, she peered into the stream to drink, but suddenly leaping to her feet, she squealed with sheer delight. "Look at me! I'm like you, but I'm so beautiful!" The thoughts of drinking from the stream and chatting with Lowey were gone from her mind like a cloud being blown by the wind. She danced up and down the embankment, skipping and twirling on two legs, "Look at me, Lowey," she called,' I'm beautifully and wonderfully made. I am so thankful to have been created and live in this Garden." As quickly as she had appeared, she was gone.

"Oh dear" thought Lowey.

Lowey sat down on the edge of the riverbank and dipped his toes into the water. He wriggled his bottom a little closer to the edge, careful not to fall in but allowing the water to rise up his little furry legs. The water soaked through the ginger curls and deep into the skin and he sighed with contentment. The air was cool, and the breeze still carried the scent of the wildflowers. In the distance he could hear Savannah's squeaks of joy as she danced and skipped her way through the ferns which were dotted along the bank, still singing praises to her Creator.

A mist had curiously formed over the stream and just seemed to be hovering there. The quiet of the Garden wrapped itself lovingly around Lowey, giving him time to think about his encounter with Savannah. How exhausted he felt by her ramblings and excitement, he stuck a small-clawed digit into his ear and wriggled it around, shaking his head he breathed in a long deep breath and slowly let it out.

"Oh my." Lowey sighed. "You most certainly do not know all things, and you do not know most things either. Who is the Giant living in the Garden? And now there is Savannah," he pondered.

"I just assumed I was the only one." A small tear glistened as it started to form in the corner of his eye; his heart felt heavy. "What a fool I am and how puffed up I have been. Savannah is like me but different, she saw the beauty and rejoiced, she was so was grateful for how she had been made, I saw the beauty and gloated. She was thankful, and I was prideful. I am so sorry," Lowey groaned. "Please forgive me," he called to the Garden. The quiet of the Garden wrapped itself more tightly around Lowey, and he was filled with a sense of peace and calm, he was genuinely sorry. "I will never say and think about those things again."

The mist over the river swirled around him, twisting and twirling this way and that as if dancing with joy. Lowey could smell something he had never smelled before, this scent was so sweet and comforting, his heart began to leap, and he felt as though he was floating on a cloud. Tears of joy rolled down his furry little cheeks, and a little sob choked in his throat. Right then and there he knew in his heart that he had indeed been forgiven and that there was something extraordinary about the Garden.

CHAPTER 2

~ ❧ ~

The Creation

S avannah had been sitting in the sunshine watching the antics of the other creatures who were continually appearing out of nowhere. To her surprise, she knew the name of each type of animal. She managed to introduce herself to a great deal of them as well. The sun was just starting to set in the distance, it had been the perfect day in the Garden. First of all, she had woken up in this magnificent place, she had met another Guinea pig called Lowey who had made her so welcome, and now the Garden was filling with so much beauty she feared it might overflow.

"Where are they all coming from?" she thought.

Only moments later, Lowey came rushing up to her, shattering her peace, he skidded a little on some leaves that had fallen from the trees.

"Savannah, I have been looking for you everywhere, you must come and see what is happening over the other side of the stream!" Lowey screeched. "Quickly, catch me if you can!" he called.

Savannah set off trying to run as fast as Lowey; he was trotting along, his bottom wiggling from side to side. Savannah managed to catch up and run alongside Lowey. His head was tilted downward, and his ears were flapping a little, his lips were set in a natural smile. Savannah burst into squeaks of laughter and fell behind; she couldn't go on any longer. She stopped and placed her little paws onto her sides, bent over and let out a sound that she didn't even know could make, it sounded like a bird chirping. By this time, Lowey had also stopped running, he had turned and was standing looking at her completely perplexed.

"What could be so funny that you would abandon our little race like that?" Lowey grumped.

"Oh, Lowey," Savannah cried holding her side, "you looked so funny running along with that smile on your face!" Lowey could not help but laugh too.

"Well," he said, "I was enjoying our race, and I won!"

"Yes, you did win, paws down!" Savannah said with a huge smile.

Lowey suddenly remembered why he had gone to find Savannah in the first place. "Savannah, I was sitting by the stream, and a pair of deer came by, do you know what deer are?" he asked.

"Yes, I saw them not too long before you found me." Savannah replied.

"I decided to go and investigate and see where these new creatures were coming from. There is a tunnel that runs under the stream and comes out into a big clearing on the other side. There are lots of fruit trees and all kinds of incredible flowers and shrubs too. I saw the Man who picked me up and named us. He was asleep. One minute he was on his own and the next moment, well there was another one, but a female, he woke up and didn't seem the least bit surprised. He spoke to the Garden and said, 'She is the flesh of my flesh and bone of my bones, I shall call her Woman!'"

"Oh, is that what happened with us? Did you fall asleep and I was made from you?" inquired Savannah.

"I'm not sure; perhaps we can go and talk to the Man and find out." Lowey replied. Savannah stood up and looked at Lowey expectantly, Lowey pointed in the direction of a big old willow tree on the bank of the river. Its branches hung low over the water and they swayed to-and-fro on the breeze.

"It's not too far from here" said Lowey, "just past the willow tree." They both wiggled along together, Savannah couldn't help but notice how handsome Lowey was; she wiggled a little closer to him and nuzzled along the side of his face. Lowey grinned. They hadn't walked too far when an opening in the ground came into view.

"I was having a look down there for somewhere to sleep and found it went all the way to the other side of the bank. Come on, I will go first, and you can follow, but stay close." Lowey whispered.

Savannah stayed close to Lowey as she started her way down into the dark hole, it smelled quite damp, and the soil underfoot was very cool. It wasn't unpleasant; it would be a lovely place to rest in the middle of the day when the sun was high in the sky. Lowey had moved on through the tunnel and was now calling to Savannah, "Come on, don't fall behind." Savannah ran a little way to catch up and felt the warmth of the sun shining through the opening. Lowey was wiggling his way up the embankment, he turned around and whispered, "Come on this way, let's try to be as quiet as we can so that we can get up close."

Savannah nodded and followed Lowey. A sizeable fallen branch covered in moss and surrounded by soft ferns made a wonderful place to hide them, and it gave them a perfect view of the clearing. Such a vast expanse of the Garden was now before them; the edges were lined with all kinds of fruit trees, and bushes filled with wild berries of every type. Lowey had to wipe the side of his mouth, how delicious everything looked. On the edge of the clearing, there was an enormous riverbank. This was the river into which the stream flowed. He nudged Savannah to direct her attention. A pair of pigeons paraded past, cooing softly to each other, and nodding their heads in Lowey's direction.

"Pigeons," Lowey said to Savannah with a big grin on his face.

"Yes," Savanah replied, "Pigeons!" They both let out a chuckle; this had now become their little joke.

The garden clearing appeared to be empty; the sky had become darker as the sun moved behind the distant mountains.

"I think we must have missed them," said Lowey; "perhaps they have found a place to sleep for the night, we should do the same, but not before we have eaten our fill of berries, come on."

The pair wiggled across the clearing, the sounds of the evening filling their ears. The cicadas were now chirping, outlines of evening creatures could be seen sitting on the rocks near the river, completely engrossed in the glory of the dragonflies that were swirling around just above the surface of the water.

Approaching the bushes, their noses were filled with the kind of smells that made their little tummies rumble loudly. The berries were a deep crimson colour and dew had started to gather on some of the leaves, they could wait no longer. Furry little digits were clinging to the leaves pulling down the small branches to pluck the tempting treats and tossing them to the ground in readiness to retrieve the next berry. Very quickly, a pile of berries began to build. Savannah noticed that no sooner had she plucked the berry and tossed it onto the pile than it was whipped away by Lowey. The red liquid was now dribbling down his chin and onto his fur. "One for me and one for the pile" he giggled.

"Lowey!!" Savannah cried "you couldn't wait for me?" Lowey stopped chewing, "there, I'm waiting."

Savannah sat down next to the pile of berries "You suit your name, you know!"

Lowey grinned and popped another berry into his mouth. "I am happy to say that I certainly do. I am the original Pig."

Finally, with full and satisfied tummies, Lowey thought that he and Savannah should find a warm and cosy spot to spend the night. Perhaps they should think about making a home nearby. Lowey remembered a little woodland area that they had passed on their way to the clearing.

Maybe in the morning they could go and have a look, but perhaps tonight they would snuggle inside the fallen branch, it was dry and just big enough to fit them both.

The sun had long gone and the night was now in all its glory. Savannah and Lowey were curled up side by side, eyes closed and both dreaming of a new day in the Garden filled with exciting adventures, foot races and bellies full of the juiciest berries.

Morning arrived quickly it seemed, the sun was just poking its head over the horizon when Lowey opened his mouth and did an enormous yawn. He licked his lips and stretched out his front legs. He looked over at Savannah and couldn't help but notice how the sun glinting on her fur was making her look almost ethereal.

Lowey thought to himself, "She is my WoPig; she is the flesh of my flesh and bone of my bones." Looking lovingly at Savannah, he let out a brrrrrrrrrrrrr sound, "Oh my goodness, what on earth was that!" Lowey wondered. He was a little surprised by how he felt. He edged forward and nuzzled her face, tickling her nose with his long white whiskers.

Poor Savannah was startled awake by Lowey's intrusion and let out a colossal wheek, leaping sideways and almost hitting her head on the roof of the log. "Lowey!! You gave me a terrible fright!" Lowey had also been thrown back with a thud when she had jumped and was now rubbing the side of his head with his paw.

"I'm sorry" Lowey cried. "Your beauty just overcame me."

This being a perfect answer for Savannah she quickly forgave him with a smile and then began to preen herself. "A girl needs to look her best at all times" she chuckled to herself.

Lowey started to walk to the end of the log and peered into the daylight, feeling it was best to leave Savannah to her preening. "Quick, the Man and the Woman are back" he called. Savannah stopped mid lick and dashed to the end of the log, her little pink tongue still poking out of her mouth. A huge squeak of delight suddenly escaped from her mouth, and before Lowey was able to say a word, Savannah was wiggling her way across the clearing, and straight up to the Woman who was standing by a tree eating a piece of fruit.

"Hello, little one" the Woman said, bending down and scooping Savannah up in her hand. "Would you like some of my fruit? You must be starving?" Savannah gingerly took the piece from the Woman's hand and held it in her little paws. It was delicious; the sweet juice dribbling from her mouth made its way down onto her soft curly fur as her enormous teeth munched away at a fast pace. Savannah swallowed and suddenly remembered what she needed to ask the Woman.

"Can you tell me if I am like you, and was I made from Lowey?" Savannah squeaked. Lowey had just arrived at the feet of the Woman, and he too was suddenly lifted into the air. One minute he was on the ground and the next he was nestled next to Savannah, in the protective grip of the Woman's hands and was being kissed on the head. Lowey tried to struggle free, "Oh Savannah, this is terrible" he squeaked. "You should have asked the Man, now look at the pickle we are in!"

"You are both so lovely!" The Woman cooed.

"Come and have a look at these guinea pigs, they are delightful."

The Man appeared at the Woman's side and stood grinning at them. "I named them first' he said, "the noise they make reminded me of a pig and look at the funny little shape of their bodies, and those short legs, they are beautiful, aren't they?"

"Did you ask the Woman the question?" Lowey asked Savannah. "I did, and I am still waiting for the answer," Savannah replied.

The Man told the Woman what The Gardener had said. "I have brought forth from the ground all the living creatures according to their kinds, livestock and creeping things and beasts of the earth. Each creature needed a name, and I have named them all!"

"Oh my!" squeaked, Lowey, "we are different from them, we were made from the earth."

The Woman smiled down at the two Guinea pigs in her hands and put them back on the ground.

Lowey couldn't help himself, he broke into a dance, bouncing all around them this way and that, wiggling his bottom and kicking out his legs. Savannah couldn't help but join in, she had no idea why, but it was such fun. The Man and the Woman were mesmerised by the antics of these two little creatures and realised what a gift they were; that they had been created to fill their hearts with love and joy.

CHAPTER 3

ஃ

The Fallen Fruit

It was morning in the Garden, and the sun shone with such brightness that the morning dew could be seen glistening in the cobwebs that were strung like decorations between the trees. Savannah sprang lightly through the grassy mounds stopping only occasionally to pluck a long strand of grass, pop it into her mouth and nibble her way to the end with such skill. She adored the sweetness of the grass, with its juicy green stems that took no time to devour.

THE FALLEN FRUIT

"Another one I think!" She sang to herself, "and another…" Savannah finished off her blade of grass and continued along the path. This part of the garden had been tended to by a Great Gardener. All He had to do was imagine the beauty, and it came into being. Lowey and Savannah often thought they had caught a glimpse of Him walking in the garden but had never actually seen him, unlike the Man and the Woman. Lowey had once heard The Great Gardener talking with them, "something about the fruit trees in the Garden," he had not heard everything, only that some trees must be left alone and that some were better than others.

"I think all fruit trees are good," Lowey had said to Savannah. "Why should one be better than the other? Maybe we can have a look next time we are the over near those trees or ask the Man." Savannah agreed, thinking to herself that she would undoubtedly find out more the next time she was with them.

She happily wiggled her way down the winding path, past the big willow tree and stopping at the stream, as the grass had now given her quite a thirst. The air was cooled down near the creek, and the moss was spongy under her little feet, how delightful was their Garden, it never ceased to provide all that they needed. With joy momentarily overwhelming her, she couldn't help doing a little leap and twist in the air.

"It is a glorious day in the Garden" she announced and landed with a thud. A movement near the willow tree alerted Savannah that she was not alone, she could see something moving slowly, it was heading towards the tunnel which ran deep under the stream and into the clearing. The new arrival also spotted Savanah and stopped moving; he was now laying very still next to a fallen log, his skin was brilliant green and glistened as the sunlight was reflected off the stream. She could see that he was a very long and slender fellow.

"Oh, it's a Serpent, it's the first one that I have seen, I will be able to tell Lowey something for a change," she giggled.

Filled with excitement, Savannah wiggled forward to get a better view of this glorious looking creature, and she lifted a paw into the air to acknowledge his presence. He didn't move from his position beside the log but shifted his enormous scaled head toward Savannah and looked directly at her.

"Hello, my name is Savannah. I live here in the garden with my Lowey and my friends the Man and the Woman" she was off again, chattering away with excitement. "Have you only just arrived in the garden?"

"Sssssssssss ssssssssssssssssss sssssssssssssssssss" hissed the Serpent "You are a funny little creature, why don't you slow down a little, come here and sit closer to me?"

The Serpent had now twisted his body away from the log and was wrapping himself around the base of the willow tree, his head rising on his long scaly neck.

"Come little one; there is nothing to fear." Savannah wiggled her way up to where he was sitting; his body was swaying in a hypnotic motion which made her feel a little uneasy, she edged close enough to look into his enormous yellow and black eyes.

"That's right," he hissed. Savannah couldn't help but notice that he kept smiling and making a sound that somewhat reminded her of a laugh, not a fun laugh but one that made her feel uneasy like he was laughing at her.

"Nowsssssssssssssssss little one, tell me where you are off to ssss? Perhaps I can accompany you on your journeysssssssssssssssssss." hissed the Serpent.

"I am on my way to visit with some dear friends, to find out about some fruit trees, the Great Gardener says some are better than others, and well, we, Lowey and I that is, don't see how that can be. We love fruit, and all fruit is good for us." Savannah announced with joy. "The Man and The Woman are the best friends in the whole garden; you will love them!" She babbled on in her squeaky little voice. The Serpent sat motionless just staring at her, trying to keep up with her ramblings. A grin started in the corner of his mouth and soon spread to the other side, and a hiss escaped from his mouth. Savannah was fascinated; she had never seen such a large mouth and stood up on her back legs to get a better look at the long-pointed tongue.

Suddenly Savannah slapped a little paw over her pink pouting lips and let out a muffled highpitched squeak. She looked at the Serpent "Oh how rude of me, I forgot to ask your name; I am so sorry, please do forgive me!"

The snake looked at Savannah, his eyes squinted, and he began to hiss, quietly at first and then louder like a slow deflating hiss, his shiny long green body began to wiggle up and down. "Oh", he giggled, "you are a funny one, my name is Nachashhhhhhhhhhhhhhhhhhh," he hissed. "Perhaps you could come a little closer and repeat that back to me so that I know that you heard me."

Savannah looked at the Serpent and moved away from him a little bit. She was now starting to feel that this new creature was very unusual and perhaps couldn't be trusted. "Thank you, Nachash" she replied, "but I heard your name."

The Serpent hissed again and began slithering towards Savannah, forcing her to wiggle backwards towards the hole. She had an overwhelming sense that she should not trust this Serpent Nachash and perhaps it was time to be on her way.

Without any warning, Lowey appeared at her side, giving her quite a fright. She wheeked at the top of her voice, lost her footing and tumbled down into the hole. Lowey couldn't believe what had happened; he simply wanted to see where she had been for so long.

"Savannah!" Lowey yelled at the top of his voice, "Are you alright?"

He had turned and was moving as fast as his little legs could take him down into the tunnel. Savannah was laying still on her side, her beautiful curls covered in mud, and she appeared to be asleep.

"Are you alright?" Lowey whispered coming closer to her face. He could feel the warm breath coming from her mouth; it was sweet smelling like the grass she had been eating. "Wheeeeeeek," Savannah screeched, leaping to her feet and bounding off down the tunnel.

Lowey squealed with delight and raced after her; "You are so mean to scare me like that!" he hollered and let out a laugh. The pair ran through the tunnel and out onto the embankment on the other side of the stream. Savannah reached a rocky outcrop and was preening her coat once again, nibbling at the mud and spitting the little bits around her feet. Lowey looked at her lovingly and shook his head; he smiled with a sense of relief that his beautiful Savannah was not injured.

"Lowey come here to me," Savannah called. Lowey trotted up to the rocks and started to scramble up, dirt and leaves flying out from behind his feet, his little woolly bottom wriggling.

"No, Lowey, not that way!" she laughed "come around the back." Lowey stopped struggling and looked down from the rock.

"Oh," he muttered. He slid back down and ran around the corner. "Now what could be so important that you would interrupt my attempt to climb up to you?" Lowey grinned. Savannah kissed Lowey lightly on the nose and looked into his eyes.

"This" she whispered, turning his head with her paws in the direction of the other side of the stream. Lowey rubbed his eye with his paw, stood up on his hind legs, and squinted through the bright sun. Far off in the distance, he could see two large human-like figures with what resembled wings, they were glowing brightly and appeared to be guarding the edge of the garden with enormous swords.

"Oh my, oh my ears!" squeaked Lowey, "I have never seen anything like that before, and, well I suppose we have always been going the other way, and we don't look back."

"What do you suppose it is?" Savannah asked.

"I'm not too sure." Lowey squeaked. He sat down on the rock next to Savannah. They had been there for quite some time pondering what appeared to be a new addition to the garden, when suddenly the sky began to darken, something they had never seen in the day. "Lowey, did you see the Serpent come out of the tunnel?" Savannah asked "I didn't, but then I don't see much when I get to preening, and my coat was very muddy" she squeaked quickly.

Lowey sat thinking for a moment, gently running his claws down along his large curly white whiskers and not letting them go for a time.

"Mmm, I don't think so," he replied. "Perhaps we just didn't notice him slithering past us. Did you find out much about him?" Savannah was about to reply when an enormous drop of water fell from the sky and landed in the middle of her head. She shook her head, spraying the water droplets in all directions and wiped her face with her two paws. Now totally distracted, Savannah turned her attention to the noise that she could hear in the distance, and the ground beneath their feet started to rumble. "What on earth is that noise, Lowey?" She squeaked. Lowey was up on all fours, with his nose sniffing the air.

"Come on; we had best go and see for ourselves" Lowey replied.

The pair set off up the embankment, through the grass and around the log which was now their home. Upon reaching the log, Lowey ensured that Savannah stayed behind him and gently shushed her with his paw. Very slowly, he crept to the edge of the log, the smell of moss and grass filled his nose, a scent that he adored, and he was momentarily distracted. "Oops, don't forget what you're doing" Lowey he muttered to himself. Securing his paw on the edge of the log he peeped around the corner into the clearing, expecting to see some wonderful kind of excitement and fun being had by the other creatures in the garden, but instead, the clearing was empty. "Oh, Savannah, nothing is happening, I wonder what all that noise was?"

The clearing was empty of its occupants. Usually, it was alive with residents enjoying the lush foliage and basking in the sunshine. Lowey and Savannah decided that perhaps they should make a little trip across to the fruit trees and find The Man and The Woman. They would know what all the commotion was.

With little bottoms wiggling in unison they trotted over to the other side of the clearing, but now had only one thing on their minds, berries! Empty tummies always took precedence over everything else, and when a bush of lush berries was spotted, well, feasting happens!! Lowey arrived first and immediately standing up on his back legs, he grasped a branch in his paws and pulled it down low enough for Savannah to pluck off a ripe red berry with her teeth. Lowey grinned at her and did the same.

"Oh, how wonderful is our life," blurted out Lowey, accidentally spitting out some of his berries, and wiping his mouth with the back of his paw. "How wonderful that we are created for each other, and how amazing is the Great Gardener that he could speak into being all this beauty!" Lowey let out a huge wheeky laugh. "Oh Savannah, I sound just like you!"

Savannah had taken absolutely no notice of Lowey and continued to stuff berry after berry into her little cheeks.

No time at all seemed to have passed since they had finished their feasting. Laying in front of the bushes, the pair were now, absolutely exhausted. Their stomachs were so full they could burst.

The two friends were filled with such satisfaction and a sleepyness that only comes with feasts of such proportion drifted over them. However, the peace was not to last for very much longer.

Within moments, Savannah and Lowey once again felt the movement of the ground around the bushes under which they had taken shelter.

Fear was something that Lowey and Savannah had never felt before, but now a strange feeling washed over them. "Savannah, I don't like how this feels." Lowey spoke in a small voice. "Perhaps we should try to find the Man and the Woman; they can tell us what is happening!" They both began pushing their way through a row of bushes; the foliage was so hard and dense that Lowey moved ahead to protect Savannah from anything that might harm her. The underneath of the bushes was dark, making it hard to see ahead, it was only then that Lowey realised that the sun had almost disappeared. "It's not time for sleep" Lowey thought, "where could the sun have gone?" He continued through, and finally, his head popped out of the underneath of the bush, and once clear, he turned and stuck his head back into the bush to help Savannah.

It was now very dark, and rumblings had started across the sky, "Oh my! Look at this!" Lowey called. Savannah couldn't believe how dark the garden was; the air had become alive with streaks of light that lit up the sky, and then soon after was followed by more rumbling and a loud crash. The Man and the Woman were nowhere to be found. Off in the distance, the ground appeared to be moving as if alive. Lowey called to Savannah to follow him and stay close; this was certainly no time to be separated. Lowey headed towards a large fruit tree, his fur was starting to stand up on end from the light in the sky, and he could feel Savannah running along-side him. "I don't know what to do! I don't know what to do!" he cried to himself. Tears were now beginning to well up in his eyes. "What is happening to our beautiful garden?" he thought. Running closer to the fruit tree,

Lowey could see something green slithering through the grass towards the great moving ground.

Coming to almost an immediate stop, Lowey grabbed Savannah's paw, "Stay here and be quiet," he whispered in her ear. Savannah was good at doing what Lowey told her, he always looked out for her and would never let anything happen to her. She was suddenly aware that these thoughts and feelings were new to her. She sat down, but that was not low enough to the ground, so she lay down. Such sadness washed over her. "Why do I feel this way?" She sobbed. Lowey returned, he lay down next to her and nuzzled her little face. Tears were running down her glistening black whiskers and onto the ground. "Oh, Savannah," Lowey purred "It's going to be alright. If we cannot find the Man and the Woman, then perhaps the Great Gardener will help us." Lowey said, trying to reassure her.

Savannah's little body was shaking, but she knew that she needed to gather all the strength she had to get up onto her feet. Struggling a little, she sat up and wiped her eyes with her two paws. Tears still dripping from the end of a whisker, she looked at Lowey and smiled. Lowey just snuggled in closer and placed his paw on hers. "That's my girl," he said and winked. Lowey was quickly becoming very apt at appearing calm, but on the inside, his heart was racing so fast he felt he might faint. "Perhaps we should just take a moment and think about what to do next," Lowey thought. Looking around, he noticed that there was a delicious red apple lying on the ground not too far from where they were resting. "The fruit has fallen from the tree" Lowey said to Savannah. "I wonder why it has fallen from the tree?" he thought. Then he noticed that it was not a whole apple and that it was mostly eaten. Looking around, Lowey decided it looked good enough to eat and grabbed it in his long sharp teeth and pulled it into their protective clutches.

Savannah was happy to eat a little something before they went to look for The Man and The Woman, as her tummy had started to get a little gnawing feeling again. Forgetting entirely about the situation they were in, they ate swiftly, one either side of the partial piece of apple. It was simply delicious, this was the best fruit they had eaten in the garden yet! Lowey couldn't help smiling, making him look very goofy, juice dripping out of the side of his mouth. "Oooh, it's just too tasty" he slurped. Suddenly overhead there was a huge crack and gigantic sheets of light broke through their newfound joy, Lowey almost choked on the piece in his mouth. He let go of the apple and yelled at Savannah "Run!" Before they knew it, they were running through the outskirts of the garden joining the moving mass of creatures who were also fleeing from the noise and light show that had taken on a life of its own above them.

Lowey broke off from the group, grabbing Savannah by the fur and tugging her as hard as he could to move her off to the side. Savannah screeched and ran alongside Lowey. They were running faster and faster; the clouds had now released their torrents of rain, and it was becoming hard to see. It was at that time that they realised that they had left the garden and were running along the outskirts, through piles of leaves which were now soaking wet. Lowey looked down and to the side, lost his footing on the side of an embankment and slipped down to the bottom on his back. He was wheeking loudly as he slid straight into a hole in the trunk of a huge tree, coming to an abrupt halt at the end of the trunk. Lowey lay on the ground holding his ears in his paws, "Oh my, oh my, oh my ears!" he wailed. Savannah suddenly leapt in through the opening and landed on Lowey with a thud.

"Lowey are you okay?" she shrieked. He was lying flat on his back with Savannah sitting on top of him; he was so thankful that he was not badly injured and hadn't met his demise. He started to roll over, and Savannah jumped off, she helped him to his feet and started fussing over him. "Not now, Savannah!" Lowey grumbled. He hobbled to the opening and peered out into the darkness, the rain was still coming down, and it was now cool outside. "It certainly is a warm and cosy hole," Lowey announced. "Perhaps we should stay here for now, see how dry it is even with all of this water?" He started moving some of the leaves and sticks that had been some sort of bedding for the previous occupant. "I hope that whoever was here before us will not return anytime soon and ask us to leave" he thought. Lowey used his little back feet to kick as much as he could to the opening to keep out the cool, while Savannah made a cosy little place for them to sleep at the back of the trunk. She waved her paw at Lowey to come and rest up with her until the sun returned once again.

Savannah was soon asleep and breathing deeply. Lowey crept from her side and moved back to the opening. What had happened? He could not believe that all the residents of the beautiful garden had run for their lives. He huffed a little when he remembered that they too had run. "Tomorrow will be a better day" he thought. "We will find the Man and the Woman, and all will be put right." Lowey moved back into the warmth of the bedding, laid his head down next to Savannah and gave his tired, sore and muddy body a final stretch before surrendering to sleep.

CHAPTER 4

The Way Back

The morning light was just beginning to filter in through the hole in the tree trunk. Small pieces of dust twisted and twirled in the air, and the red and orange of the leaves glowed brightly. What had started as a little, warm and cosy bed had now grown into a mountainous nest which filled almost the entire corner of the tree trunk. Now and then the leaves would rustle a little, and a small pink foot would stretch out into view. A curious dance began, the leaves would rustle and move about and then a foot would quickly shoot out of the leaves and then be pulled back in almost as soon as it appeared. Anyone watching at the entrance would undoubtedly have been confused by this peculiarity.

Lowey yawned and stretched a foot as far as it would go and then stretched the other. "Ahh!" he sighed. He noticed that he had a rather sore front paw which made him wheek with pain when he stretched it out in front.

"What's the matter, Lowey?" Savannah mumbled.

"I have a very sore paw; I must have fallen on it when I slipped last night" Lowey told Savannah. All the memories of the day began to flood back, and Lowey felt a sense of sadness overwhelm him. Savannah popped her head out through the top of the pile of crunchy leaves, her shiny black whiskers moving up and down as she sniffed the cool morning air. Noticing that the entry was almost blocked, she shuffled down to the floor and started scratching at the ground and pulling at the leaves and twigs to make an opening.

"Lowey, look at all of the leaves; the wind must have blown them all in during the night, come and help me move them out of the way. We are going to need to go outside and find out what has become of the creatures that left the garden. I wonder if we can go back to the garden now, I don't want to have to stay out here."

Lowey interrupted Savannah's ramblings with a noise that made her stop and listen immediately. Savannah turned to see Lowey standing up as tall as he could, his back arched, and his teeth were making a chattering noise. Instantly Savannah was at Lowey's side, his teeth were clanking together as though he was cold, it was a sound that she had never heard before, but it was one that resonated with her, and she knew that something was not well with their world.

Savannah had been babbling away as usual when Lowey had felt a tap on his back. Turning around, he was confronted with an intruder! Lowey could not believe his eyes; another Guinea pig stood facing him, standing tall and proud. Lowey had no control over the response, and Savannah was at his side as though she knew something was wrong. Lowey was rather impressed by the natural way they just fell into unison and was, as usual, momentarily distracted by that thought.

Shaking his head, Lowey looked at the newcomer and decided that introductions were probably by now, quite overdue.

"My name is Lowey, and I am the, I am the?" Lowey had no idea who he was anymore; he certainly was not the Knower of most things in the garden; nothing made any sense now.

"My name is Lowey, and this is my, Savannah" he announced and then moving closer to Savannah, he stared up at the new Guinea pig and followed it up with another rumble which worked its way out of his mouth without any assistance. "And who might you be?" Lowey squeaked, feeling somewhat uneasy by the intrusion.

"Good morning to you sir, I say, good morning," he smiled at Lowey and shot a small wink at Savannah, making Lowey rumble again. "My name is Avery, my good sir, and this," and without any warning, a little fuzzy head appeared from behind Avery, "is Constance" he finished.

Savannah was suddenly hopping from one foot to another and squeaking with joy. The intruder, Avery, had brought a friend it appeared, which delighted Savannah no end.

Everything inside the tree trunk had momentarily shifted into slow motion for Lowey; he was standing on all fours, glued to the spot watching everything unfold in front of him. Savannah had finished bouncing around behind Lowey and had moved to introduce herself to Constance.

Avery appeared to be amused by the whole thing and was leaning against the wall of the trunk snickering to himself. Lowey felt nothing but resentment. "Who was this intruding upstart?" he wondered. He began to size up Avery. He was certainly enormous in stature, much larger than Lowey and stood a good inch taller, he surmised. His fur was nowhere near as lovely as Lowey's and it was the colour of an early sunrise, smooth and sleek and it clung to his body showing every lump and bump. "Nothing left to the imagination" Lowey smirked to himself, "eat a few too many berries, and everyone will notice!" Avery had enormous black eyes, smaller whiskers around the top of his nose, and long sleek white ones on his cheeks. His head was kissed with a streak of black which ran down the middle of his back. He was, in fact, quite a handsome chap, although Lowey didn't want to admit it.

Finally snapping back into reality, Lowey wobbled over to Avery and lifting his head high enough to touch the whiskery nose he noticed that Avery had a tooth missing. On closer inspection, Lowey could see that Avery had not escaped the great moving herds as well as he and Savannah had.

"What is this?" grumbled Lowey. "How is it that you came to be in our fine abode this morning without even an invitation? And who is Constance?" Once again, Lowey was reminded about how much like Savannah he sounded!

"One question at a time old chap!" said Avery with a grin. Lowey could see the gap where the tooth had been.

"Yes, of course" Lowey replied, feeling a bit rotten.

By this time Savannah was happily chattering away with Constance. "What a poor bedraggled little creature she is" Lowey thought. Constance was very petite, unlike her companion, however, she too had a sleek, shiny coat that hugged her body outlining her fine frame. It was a beautiful mix of black, white and browns, and an enormous crest adorned her head. Her eyes were large and wide open as though she had been given a fright, and her lips, oh such beautiful pink and pouting lips. Lowey noticed that she also had not faired too well, her ear had been torn on one side and it drooped downwards a little, some of her whiskers were missing, and a large patch of hair had been torn from her front foot.

Lowey instantly decided that he and Savannah should help Avery and Constance; after all, there was safety in numbers.

"Right!" Lowey said happily. "Let's move these leaves from the opening and see what this day has in store for us."

"A jolly good idea, Lowey!" Avery added, and slapped him on the back with his large paw, jolting Lowey forward. It was going to take some time to get used to Avery, Lowey realised. At once, Savannah and Constance headed toward the opening, moving the leaves and debris out of the way, their little paws working their way through to the outside. Before they knew it, the light was streaming in through the hole. Both girls attempted to push through to the outside at the same time and banged their heads. Savannah squeaked with laughter, rubbing the top of her head with her paw, and moved back out of the way to let Constance pass.

Moments later, standing in front of the great tree trunk, they surveyed very different surroundings. Lowey looked up to the large embankment and grimaced a little, remembering his slippery journey down its steep slope. The ground was covered in broken branches, leaves and flowers had been torn from their homes, and some of the trees had been pulled clean out of the ground and were lying with their roots in the air. They stood looking at the devastation, unable to speak.

It was finally Savannah who broke the silence.

"Well, we will need to find a way to the top of the bank to see if we can return to the garden" Savannah said. "The Great Gardener will be so worried about us all."

It was then that they all realised that they had not felt nor heard the Great Gardener for some time now. "What could have happened yesterday?" Lowey thought.

Nodding her head, Constance agreed. "I just want to go home" she squeaked in a quiet little voice. Savannah shuffled over to her and nuzzled her face. "Don't worry, Lowey will take us back to the garden, you just wait and see." Constance looked around to see if Avery was close. "You know," Constance said, "Avery is very good at taking care of me too, he is just a bit fussy that's all" she said, pouting her lips into a kiss. Savannah giggled and pouted her lips into a kiss as well, although she had no idea what Constance had meant.

Avery and Lowey had already set off up the steep hill, slipping and sliding this way and that. The ground was thick and sticky, a mixture of grass, leaves and water mixed into the mud, and it sent shivers up their legs as it squished between their toes. Avery had stopped to shake the mud from his back foot and almost lost his footing, only just managing to grab hold of the woolly fur on Lowey's back, causing him cry out.

Avery steadied himself, "Come on ladies," he called out, looking over his shoulder. "Just you take it nice and slow, and you will be fine." Savannah was moving very gingerly up the hill with Constance close behind, when suddenly, Savannah slipped in the mud, lost her footing and slid back into Constance who tried desperately to move out of the way, but to no avail. The pair tumbled down the hill, legs flailing about and loud squeaks filling the air, and soon they landed back at the bottom of the hill.

Lowey couldn't believe what had happened, and after checking to see that the girls were okay, he shook his head then continued his way up the hill, grunting as he went. Avery was still attached to his back and had no intention of letting go. "Avery will you please let go of me?" Lowey grumbled at him.

"Indeed, old chap, I'm just steadying myself, you wouldn't want me to take a tumble like the ladies, now would you?" Avery replied.

Lowey felt as though his heart would burst as they finally reached the top of the embankment, Avery had now managed to steady himself and followed close behind. The girls were back on the move again and had nearly caught up.

Finally sitting on the top of the embankment they could see for miles. It was incredible, off to one side there was a giant river which split into four, twisting and turning on past mountains and rolling hills. Was this a part of their beautiful garden? The four little souls sat on that hill taking it all in, the bright sun shone down, warming their backs, and for the first time in a couple of days, they felt at peace once again.

Lowey moved closer to Savannah and rested his head on her back, "Are you okay?" he whispered.

Savannah pouted her lips and shot him an air kiss, Lowey was a little surprised, he had no idea what she had just done, and tilted his little fuzzy head to one side, tickling her with his big white whiskers as he did. "Oh, it's something Constance showed me" she said and repeated the action. Lowey just shook his head "Oh my ears!!" he laughed.

CHAPTER 5

A Way Back Home

The climb up the hill had exhausted everyone. Within moments of settling into the sun, just a little way back from the edge of the embankment they slept, all huddled together, a mash of colours, fluff and whiskers, chests rising and falling in time with each other.

Constance was the first to stir. Her little belly had been growling for quite some time, even before the great climb up the hill, but now she needed to find some food. Getting to her feet she moved away from the group and headed toward some bramble bushes, but they were empty.

Standing still, she could smell that the berries were quite near, and wondered why nobody else had sensed them too. Leaving the brambles, she spotted a tree which was adorned with unusually sizeable red fruit; they were very different from the berries that were growing in the garden.

Constance sat in front of one of the pieces of fruit and looked at it; she tapped it with her paw curiously; it was very hard and sounded hollow.

"Oh, this just won't do" she whined. She stood up on her back legs and grasped the fruit with her front paws and pulled. To her surprise, the fruit came away from the branch very easily and slipped onto the ground in front of her. She tapped at it with her paw, again and again. It certainly was hollow, but didn't give way under her pats. Pushing the round ball against the bush to hold it still, Constance now grasped it with both paws and bit at it with her front teeth. To her amazement a hole appeared, she bit again and again until she was able to see something glistening inside. The berries were hidden inside the fruit; they glistened pink and red and looked back at her invitingly. The scent of the berries filled her nose and she breathed deeply, "Oh what a delicious fragrance." As Constance was about to extract one of the berries, the rest of the group arrived, noses in the air, being led by the scent of the fruit.

"My, oh my, tummy," Lowey chirped, "have you tasted the fruit yet?" he asked Constance. Silence. Lowey just shook his head. Constance now had her head deep inside the shell of the fruit and her little bottom up in the air. "Oh my!" Lowey laughed. "Come on Savannah, help me get one these things down. This is a Pomegranate!" he said,

"Yes Lowey, even outside of the garden you are still the Knower!" Savannah giggled. Finally, with a sense of contentment, everyone sat looking at the pile of leftover scraps from the outside of the fruit, only a few little pink glistening gems left on the ground.

Avery looked up at the trees and beyond to where he was sure the edge of the garden had been. He scratched his head and continued to look up. Twisting his mouth a little and wiggling his whiskers he began to speak.

"I say, does anyone think it rather strange that the garden is no longer where it should be?" Everyone looked up in the same direction, and Lowey pushed a few scraps away from himself with his foot and stood up. He began walking up and down along the row of fruit trees, stopping and peering through to the brambles that were behind.

"Well, I am sure this is where Savannah and I came through, because this is the hill that I slid down and into the tree trunk." Savannah was nodding her head up and down and agreeing with a few loud wheeks. "Perhaps we should split up and explore the ridge, see if we can find an opening," Lowey suggested.

Agreeing, it was decided that Lowey and Savannah should explore to the east and Avery and Constance to the west. "Let's make sure that we return to this spot before the sun goes down; we don't want to be out in the dark and not be able to find out way home" Savannah said. This was the wrong thing to say as Constance began to whimper. "Come on now, Lassie" Avery said, tossing her a toothy grin, "there's no cause for alarm, I'll keep you safe" and he blew her an air kiss, making her smile.

Lowey and Savannah had been walking for quite some time, and the sun was starting to sink a little, feeling rather tired they sat down in the shade of some bushes. Suddenly, Savannah's ears pricked up as a familiar sound floated on the air. She moved towards the brambles and put her ear as close as she could without getting her fur caught on the thorns. "Oh, listen Lowey! It's the stream!" She could hear the babbling, she knew that sound so well, it used to sing her to sleep at night, oh how she missed that sound. It seemed to soothe her immediately, and she started to feel the peace of the Garden, wrapping itself around her once again. "Oh, Lowey" she purred, "we're home."

"Now, let's not get too excited" Lowey puffed, coming alongside her. "Let me listen." Lowey pushed in next to Savannah, and suddenly he also was overcome with the kind of peace that only the quiet in the garden could bring. A huge sigh left his lips, and he began to relax. "You are right." He too felt the peace and the joy start to stir within him, a desire to be home with the Great Gardener.

They stayed there, lying on the ground in a cocoon of warmth and love for as long as they dared, then gradually they sat up together. "We must find our way back in" Lowey said. "We can't stay out here; it just doesn't feel right."

A little further down from where they were sitting Lowey spied a hollow in the ground that would make a perfect place to spend the night. It was surrounded by tall grass which would give some protection should it come to that. Lowey decided that he would return to the place on the hill where they were to meet back up with Avery and Constance. "You stay here, Savannah, the burrow will give you some shelter, and there is plenty of grasses to eat." Savannah nuzzled Lowey's nose and then dashed behind the tall grass and disappeared out of sight.

Lowey was running as fast as his little legs would carry him, all the time watching for any break in the brambles which would reveal an opening, but at the same time being careful not to slip down the embankment like he had the day before. "Oh my, oh my, oh my poor old feet" he thought. The rough ground was starting to take its toll on his little pink feet, the ground in the garden had been soft and lush, but outside of the Garden, the ground was hard and stony. As luck would have it, Avery and Constance had returned to the bushes and were once again feasting.

Avery waved a paw at Lowey and beckoned him to come and sit. Lowey took no time in sitting down with the pair. Catching his breath, he picked up a berry from the ground and popped it into his mouth; the juice was sweet and cold on his throat as it went down. Lowey had been so engrossed in looking for a way into the garden that he had not noticed his thirst.

"Oh, that is so good" Lowey muttered as he popped another one into his mouth. Then he remembered the good news that he had to tell them. "We found the stream, we heard and felt it on the other side of the high wall, Savannah and I. We felt the quiet of the Garden." Unexpectedly, Lowey began to cry. Avery and Constance both sat looking at Lowey a little confused.

"Well you see," Lowey told them, "I have always had a connection with the Great Gardener, He revealed himself to me on that first day. The quiet in the Garden, it wraps itself around me and sinks into my heart and soul, He tells me things without speaking." Lowey couldn't help but place a little paw onto his heart. Avery and Constance still sat looking at him without saying a word. Lowey continued, "The Great Gardener fills me with such peace, and He tells me things, but he uses the quiet in the Garden, His Spirit." Lowey looked lovingly at his new friends and smiled, feeling a sense of joy that he had been able to share the good news that he had learned.

"Right! Excellent work, my good Man" Avery squeaked. He was lying on his side, sticking his paw into the gap where his tooth had been. "Do you suppose that if we can get back into the garden, that the Great Gardener would give me a new tooth?"

"I'm sure he will, Avery! The Great Gardener will say, Let there be a tooth, and it will appear, and it will be good!" Lowey grinned, Avery clapped his paws together with delight. Distraction comes in all forms for a Guinea pig: food, thoughts, and sounds!

Lowey suddenly remembered and continued to tell his companions about the burrow where he had left Savannah, and that she was waiting for them to return. "Tomorrow we can explore further and find the entrance back into the garden!" Constance said excitedly.

Lowey was about to suggest that they start back on the journey to join up with Savannah when the ground began to make a low rumbling sound. It was not as loud as the rumblings of the day before but it certainly felt like something was on the move nearby. Letting out a huge wheek Lowey began to run as fast as he could back down the hill toward the safety of the tree trunk, leaving a trail of dust in the air behind him which flew straight into Avery's eyes. "Slow down old chap" Avery shrieked. Lowey skidded into the hole followed by Avery and Constance. With their little hearts pounding, they huddled in the entrance to get a better look at what was happening now. Constance was behind the boys and was nursing her paw; she winced a little as she began licking the dirt off the fur that remained around the wound.

Lowey couldn't believe his eyes; it was the Man and the Woman; they were running along the top of the ridge and appeared to be looking for something as well.

Lowey squeaked with delight, "They're here! The Man and the Woman, all will be well now!"

Lowey shot out of the hole at top speed, charging up the hill, squeaking as loud as he could. "I'm here, I'm here!" he cried.

The more he ran, the less he could call to them, and before he even reached the top of the hill, they were out of sight, but that didn't stop him. He tucked in his head and ran as fast as he could along the top, in the same direction that he had been with Savannah. Lowey hoped that Savannah would hear them coming and leave the protection of the burrow, but the light was starting to fade, and he feared she would stay put.

"Oh, please Savannah, hear them coming and stop them!" he cried to himself.

Within moments Avery ran alongside Lowey, tugging at his fur with his three remaining teeth trying to stop him from running. Slowing down a little, Lowey grimaced at Avery, shot out his back leg and pushed him away with foot, sending Avery tumbling in a heap. Lowey kept running without looking back; he didn't have time for Avery and his silliness, he had to get to Savannah.

Slowing his pace, he recognised the space in the brambles where he and Savannah had encountered the Spirit in the Garden, and he ran toward the burrow a little further down.

He was squeaking as loud as he could for her to hear him.

"It's alright Savannah, I'm back, I'm back! Are you okay?" Silence followed. He pushed his body as hard as he could through the prominent tufts of grass that surrounded the hole, and he peered into the darkness. It smelt dank and musty, he called out again, but there was still no answer. His eyes began to adjust to the darkness, and he could see that the burrow was empty. Avery had now caught up and hobbled up behind Lowey.

"Listen here old chap! That was bad form kicking me like that." Lowey shot him an angry look, and an unconvincing apology tumbled out of his mouth.

"Now is not the time for pleasantries! Savannah's not in the hole!" he cried.

Avery stuck his enormous head into the hole and pulling it out again, he looked at Lowey. "Nope, she's not there," he said.

Lowey was starting to feel the fear rising inside of him. His skin beneath the fur was beginning to feel cold, and his heart was beating so fast he thought it would come right out of his chest.

"Think Lowey, think, where could she be? The Woman and the Man, they might have found her and taken her along with them, yes that is what has happened!"

Avery had returned to the hole and now had his entire body inside except for his legs and bottom which was wiggling. Lowey could hear his muffled voice "Yes, yes, this is very peculiar, very peculiar indeed!"

Avery shuffled backwards and emerged from the hole, his sleek fur muddied a little, and on the end of his whiskers, something was glistening in the moonlight.

"What is peculiar?" Lowey asked, stretching up to look at Avery's whiskers and sniffing. Shaking his head and then nodding in the direction of the hole, Avery placed a paw on Lowey's back, "in the burrow, right at the back it looked like, um some fur, and…" He wiped his whiskers with his massive paw and showed Lowey the sticky red liquid.

Lowey recoiled at the sight. "No! That can't be!" he wailed. "She has to be safe, she has to be! The Man and the Woman, they would have taken her with them."

Lowey sank to the ground in despair. His eyes filling with torrents of warm salty tears, which began cascading like a waterfall off the end of his nose. "She was safe in the burrow," he sobbed. "I told her she would be safe, and I would be back for her." His body shook as he thought about his beautiful Savannah and the harm that may have befallen her. Avery came alongside and nuzzled his face, and, for the first time in days having nothing to say, he snuggled in closer to Lowey and wept.

They lay exhausted on the damp ground for quite some time, hidden by the safety of the tall grass. Lowey looked up into the night sky and remembered the evenings that he and Savannah had laid upon the great rock near their home in the garden and tried to count the stars. Some nights the sky would be filled with stars that shot across the heavens, lighting up the sky with their fiery tails. Lowey shuddered with a sigh and wiped the tears away with his small paw. How he longed to be back again safe and secure in their garden.

Lowey was so thankful that Avery was with him and that he was not alone, then he remembered that they had left Constance back at the tree trunk. She would probably be scared. Sitting up slowly, Lowey touched Avery on the paw. "Avery, we have left Constance alone too long, we need to return to the tree trunk." Avery stretched his body and yawned, "All right old chap," he said, "are you going to be alright leaving the burrow? What if Savannah returns, maybe you should stay here, and I'll go back." Lowey knew deep down that Savannah was not coming back to the burrow; whatever had happened, she was long gone.

As Avery and Lowey walked back along the top of the embankment, the moon floated high overhead lighting up their way. A cool breeze had picked up, blowing through the fur on top of Lowey's head and making him shiver.

Lowey felt like the journey back to the hill seemed to go on and on, each step felt like a defeat, each step took him further from Savannah, his feet were heavy like his heart, and he trudged along beside Avery. They finally arrived at the tree, "Oh how wonderful to be back" Lowey thought. As usual, Constance was chattering away as they entered the safety of the tree trunk, "Oh, finally you have come back" she said blowing Avery an air kiss and threw a glance over her shoulder smiling. Lowey moved towards Constance and looked beyond her toward the corner of the trunk.

"Oh my, oh my, oh my dear!" he squeaked. There in the corner in the warm cosy nest that they had left earlier that day, was Savannah, safe and sound. Curled up next to her were two of the tiniest little piggies that Lowey had ever seen. Lowey was speechless, he stood glued to the ground and only found his voice as Avery and Constance wheeked around the trunk, leaping and twisting with sheer joy!!

"Oh Savannah, I thought I had lost you!" Lowey cried. "How is this possible? We saw the burrow, and we thought..." his words broke off as he put his head in his paws and wept tears of joy.

Savannah left the nest, limping over to Lowey. "It's all okay now Lowey, look you are a papa." She gently nudged Lowey towards the nest and nuzzled into his side. "We are a family now, we have two little boys, and we have the Man and the Woman to thank. They saved me, Lowey."

Up on top of the hill, the Man and the Woman sat looking down upon the valley, this would be their home now, and there was no way to return to the Garden. It was time to start again, and they had begun with saving the little creature and her babies. The moon was just bedding down, and the sun was rising in the distance. The Man looked lovingly at the Woman and said, "I will call you Eve, and you will be the mother of all the living."

CHAPTER 6

Morton

Back in the tree trunk Savannah was snuggled into the warmth of the nest and encircled her two little bundles of fur and whiskers. Lowey lay alongside her, his nose as close to the little ones as possible. Savannah was sleeping, breathing deeply. She looked so peaceful, and yet so exhausted at the same. Everything had happened so quickly over the last few days. The great Exodus from the Garden, the storms and the devastation, and their beautiful garden with its impenetrable wall of brambles that had sprung up overnight, making their way back seem impossible. It was all whirling around in Lowey's head, confusing him even more than he already was. Savannah had fallen asleep not long after they had returned, telling Lowey only that the Man and the Woman had saved her and the pups. He had no idea what had happened and felt it best not to press her for more details until they had all rested. There was time enough to hear her story later.

Lowey could not stop looking at the little pups, they were the tiniest little creatures he had seen, apart from some of the smaller creatures who lived in and around the stream, of course. He was very thankful on this occasion that he didn't know most things, how these little ones came into this world was a mystery, and he was happy for it to stay that way! He sniffed at the soft baby fur; they smelt like leaves and Savannah, his heart swelled a little and warmed with such love. "We have created these little ones, Savannah!" he thought to himself. He closed his eyes and let himself drift off into a land beyond this one and in the dream, he was back in the garden.

After only being asleep for a short time, Lowey was dragged from his slumber by a strange noise.

"Oh my, oh my ears," he said sleepily. "What is all that ruckus? I'm not going to be able to fall back to sleep!" he thought. Lowey turned around to face the opposite side of the tree trunk, Avery and Constance were also curled up on another nest of leaves that Constance had roughly pushed together earlier.

Lowey lay on his side, occasionally scratching at his fur which had certainly seen better days; little pieces of twigs and mud had become knotted at the back of his legs which pulled at his skin when he stood up, a job that perhaps Savannah might help him with, he thought. The noise continued, on and off for a while. Still, everyone else continued to sleep peacefully, everyone except Lowey, who now had his little paws over his ears and his eyes shut tight trying to fall back to sleep.

Lowey finally sat up, and waddled over to the opening. Looking out into the clearing, which also needed some tending to, he gave himself a good shake. With a little leap into the air for good measure, he decided to leave the tree and return to the ridge at the top of the hill and continue to search for an opening that might lead back into the garden. He might find out where the annoying noise was coming from at the same time.

Lowey walked for a little way to the East and was intrigued by the noise; it was a sound that was usually heard at night, a loud hooting noise. In the distance, Lowey could see a group of beautiful cedar trees and in the branches of one, a bird was thrashing around.

Lowey ran as fast as his wiggle would allow, he even forgot about the annoying mat in his rear end which was making walking a bit of an effort.

"An Owl, Oh my, oh my ears!" Lowey exclaimed, he had never seen an animal of such beauty, and even as the owl was thrashing about, Lowey could see what a magnificent creature he was. He stood at least four guinea pigs higher than Lowey and was endowed with feathers of shades of many colours: blacks, browns, oranges and whites, and the tail feathers, almost striped like the markings of a tiger. The detail was not to be believed, his face was square shaped with enormous yellow and black piercing eyes, and around the eyes, large circles of orange feathers outlined the cheeks. The beak, sharp, pointed and almost hidden at the top by fluffy cream downy feathers would almost certainly be a handy tool.

"You are indeed fearfully and wonderfully made! How amazing is The Great Gardener to have imagined such a creature as you!" Lowey called out to the owl, who had now stopped thrashing about and was glaring intently at Lowey, his feathered ears on top of his head were pulled back as though he might pounce if he were not caught in the branches.

"Hoo, hoo! Help me please!" the owl cried out in desperation.

Lowey ran to the base of the tree, wondering how he was going to be able to help the poor owl.

"Just keep still and stop thrashing about, you will make things worse if you don't keep still!" Lowey squeaked.

"Please help me; my foot has been caught between these two branches for so long" the owl sobbed loudly.

Moving carefully around the tree, Lowey inspected the trunk for a way inside that might lead up and out onto a branch, but it was sealed entirely without a single opening. The owl had stopped struggling and was sitting back on the branch nursing a sore wing and looking very sorry for himself. Lowey sat down near the wall of brambles and plucked a blade of sundried grass from a mound and nibbled at it with his front teeth. Momentarily he thought of Avery's request for a new tooth. He shook his head as if trying to remove the thought and popped his pointed digit into his ear and gave it a quick wriggle. "Come on, Lowey think!" he muttered to himself. "I am after all, the Knower of most things!!"

Leaning back against the brambles, he began to rub his fur in the middle of his back against the thorns to relieve an itch that had now worked its way from his shoulder. Lowey sighed, and finishing the piece of grass, he plucked another one, popped it into his mouth and continued to think. Lowey had pushed even closer to the brambles, now that feeling of closeness to the Garden began to envelop him. Lowey closed his eyes tight, clasped his little paws together and spoke into the air around him, "Oh Great Gardener, you are the Knower of everything, you spoke all of this into being, and I am so grateful for all that you have done and continue to do. Still, I am so lost and am not sure how to help this poor soul."

The owl leaned over the branch and was glaring at Lowey with his piercing yellow eyes; a growl began to rumble out of its beak. "Why are you speaking to the air?" He hooted at the top of his voice. "Who, who are you talking too? I'm stuck in this tree, and you are having a rest, a bite to eat and talking to the air! While I am suffering."

Lowey continued to ignore the Owl's outburst, and gripped his little paws more tightly together. He had become surrounded by the Spirit of the Garden once again and could feel its connection drawing him closer to the Great Gardener, the tears that always accompanied his arrival flowed freely. Lowey felt reassured that all would be well. Lowey opened his eyes and wiped away the tears with the back of his paw, as the owl continued to peer at him.

Getting back to his feet Lowey wiggled his way over to the trunk of the tree and stopped, suddenly standing up on two feet he patted the trunk with both of his paws, then patted it again for good measure. Lowey backed away from the trunk and looked up at the confused owl.

"Just stay still" Lowey called to the owl. "The Great Gardener has assured me that all will be well."

The owl was about to strongly object, when the branch he was perched on cracked clean in two. Slipping down onto the next branch, his foot that had been in its vice-like grip was finally free.

Now free at last, he flapped his exhausted wings and fluttered to the ground, landing in front of Lowey who was preoccupied with his ear once again.

Lowey was still staring at the broken branch in front of him, when the owl landed. "Oh my, oh my ears!" Lowey squeaked and jumped out of the way. Turning his attention to the injured and disgruntled owl, Lowey wiggled over to him and enquired if he was okay.

"Fine! Do I look okay to you?" the owl shot back at Lowey. "Ohhh, my foot! My wing!" he was now hopping around in a circle on one foot, his enormous wings outstretched.

Lowey had no idea how the branch had just broken; all he did was pat the tree a couple of times while he was wondering what the Great Gardener was going to do to help the owl. The angry owl was still dancing about as Lowey cleared his throat with a high-pitched squeak and catching his attention. "Let's just calm down a little and take a look at that foot," Lowey said, looking up at the owl.

The owl stopped flapping about and rested on the ground. Lowey wiggled over and was surprised by the enormity of the huge scaly foot; adorned with four large toes, each with a long shiny black claw. The perfectly formed brown feathers ran smoothly down his leg and only just reached the foot, and then soft fluffy cream coloured feathers covered the toes. Lowey was taken back by the sheer beauty of the Great Gardener's work in this creature. Lowey looked up at the owl; his lips open a little, his paw once again found its way to his ear which he immediately began to scratch. "You are fearfully and wonderfully made," Lowey announced. The owl pushed himself up from his position on the ground and balanced on the one uninjured foot. "Yes, yes I am" he chirped smiling down at Lowey, "Morton is my name, and…" before he could finish his sentence, Lowey blurted out, "You're a Great Horned Owl! And I am Lowey."

"What did you do to the tree?" Morton asked, ignoring Loweys outburst.

"I asked the Great Gardener what to do, and he said that all would be well and…"

Lowey suddenly stopped mid-sentence, his heart started to beat a little faster, and he felt joy welling up inside of his stomach. "It was the Great Gardener!" Lowey wheeked excitedly. "He pruned the tree, don't you see?? Before Morton could comment, Lowey was leaping into the air and wiggling his bottom about, landing on all fours and somersaulting. He couldn't help it; the joy was bubbling out of him.

Lowey shook himself off and sat down in front of Morton who was by now completely confused by the dance that Lowey had just performed. Lowey sat quietly while Morton stood up and began attending to his foot. Suddenly, Lowey was acutely aware of the reason he was continually being drawn back up the hill, it was the Spirit in the Garden, and he felt an overwhelming sense of wellbeing.

Lowey suddenly remembered Savannah and the pups, and a funny sickness tickled his tummy momentarily. He realised it was probably best to be on his way back to the tree trunk.

Lowey looked over to Morton, who was sitting back down again rubbing his injured foot with his beak. "I do believe the damage is not too bad, and besides, I can still fly," he said with a laugh.

"Where are you nesting?" Lowey asked, thinking about how much he had enjoyed the adventure.

"I haven't found a home yet, and I can't fly high enough to return to the garden." Morton sighed. "What about you? I assume you settled nearby?"

As Lowey and Morton slowly made their back along the ridge and down the hill to the tree, Lowey explained how he and Savannah had found their new home and about Avery and Constance. "We're a family now" Lowey thought. "Perhaps you would like to settle with us? Maybe there is another hole further up in the tree that might serve you well as a home?" He asked Morton. Right there at that moment, Lowey knew in his heart that he was truly home and that he would never leave the Garden walls.

Later that evening, when the world was quiet, and the occupants were sleeping soundly, Lowey walked out into the clearing near the tree trunk. There was a coolness in the air, and a silver sliver of moon hung precariously in the night sky. Lowey looked around and surveyed his new home, there was a clearing, not unlike the one in the garden, and far off in the distance the rushing of the water from the river could be heard. It is perfect, we will make a home away from our old home, and we will never be far from The Great Gardener.

Lowey sat back on his haunches and pulled his little furry paws together in front of his face, closing his little back eyes. He leant on his paws, breathed in and felt the Spirit of Garden envelop him. He felt it swirling around warming his body, and his fur stood on end a little in anticipation. Lowey heard the words in his heart, not his ears, "I will never leave you, Lowey."

"Oh my, oh my heart!" Lowey whispered into the breeze.

CHAPTER 7

❦

Savannah

Morton shifted his weight onto his right foot and gave his head a shake. A breeze had picked up and was coming in off the river, ruffling the feathers of his tail and sending a shiver up his back. Reluctantly he opened an eye and peered quickly out of the hole. "Surely it can't be time to wake up just yet?" He thought.

SAVANNAH

Lowey and Savannah had been so kind as to invite Morton to settle in the tree with them and had pointed out an opening two-thirds of the way up that might be a suitable home for him. Instantly Morton had flown up and had a look inside, it was perfect and looked as though it had not been previously occupied. It had been an exhausting day being caught and injured up on the hill, so he had decided to rest up for a while now that he did not have to concern himself with finding a place to stay.

The tree gave Morton a wonderful view of the clearing and beyond the woods to the river, and he could almost see the top of the wall around the garden. It was perfect, the hole was quite deep and would make a warm and safe nest once he had lined it with leaves and twigs. He thought that perhaps some feathers would make a nice touch, but that would have to wait, he was exhausted. He snuggled back down inside the hole and closed his eyes; he was undoubtedly never awake in the light of day. Feeling sleep coming, he closed his eyes and let out a gentle sigh.

Down below, Lowey was sitting upon a massive grey rock not too far from the tree. It was so warm in the sun, and the grass around the rock was easy to nibble at without a lot of effort, and after the day that he had endured, food which required little effort was perfect.

Savannah appeared at the base of the rock and called out to Lowey quietly, pulling Lowey out of his peaceful sojourn. Lowey called back and shuffled to the edge of the rock. Savannah had started to climb up onto the rock, and they bumped noses, giving them both quite a start. Lowey jumped back, and Savannah followed with a little shake of her back and kicking her legs out.

Lowey lay back down, and Savannah snuggled in next to him.

"The little ones are asleep, and Constance is watching over them." Savannah told him.

"Lowey, do you want to know what happened upon the ridge the last night?" she asked, looking down at the rock. Her ears had fallen forward, and she sat back and wiped her face with both her paws and shook her head, setting her ears back in place.

Lowey smiled, even now, after all, that had happened, she was preening herself. Lowey felt truly blessed just by watching her; she was a magnificent creature. Lowey sat up and looked at her. "Tell me what happened Savannah, tell me everything."

So Savannah began to recall the events of the previous night.

The air had begun to cool, bringing with it the late afternoon sun which filtered through the foliage, providing light into the burrow where Savannah was waiting. The burrow smelled of rich metallic soil, reminding her of the warm log that she had shared with Lowey in The Garden, thankfully, now giving her a sense of peace.

After some time, Savannah slowly moved to the entrance of the burrow and peered out into the late afternoon. She sat quietly in anticipation of Lowey's return and was grateful to be hidden by the mounds of tall grass. She sat up on her back feet, preening the fur on her rather round belly, a little tickling sensation made her smile. Lately, she had noticed that her tummy had become rather large. At first, she thought that the many berry feasts were the cause, but now she was aware of new life growing within her. There had been no time to tell Lowey what with the great Exodus from the Garden, then the arrival of Avery and Constance.

"I must tell Lowey soon that we will be expecting new arrivals, he will be so surprised!" she thought to herself. "And we will need to prepare the nest, perhaps Constance will help?" She giggled to her belly.

After what seemed like no time at all, Savannah became aware that evening was fast approaching, and she began to worry that Lowey had not managed to make it back to the ridge in time, or that perhaps Avery and

Constance had not returned. Resigned to spending the night alone in the burrow, Savannah waddled to the grassy mound and began to break off blades of the dry outer grass, and pull them into the burrow. It took her several trips to drag enough grass inside.

A feeling of hunger had now come over her, so she wiggled down in front of a grassy mound and pushed her face right into the clump, stretching as far as she could, leaving only her bottom outside of the mound. Her whiskers tickled from the stickiness of the new shoots in the centre of the grass. She nibbled at them with her front teeth. They were so sweet, "like fresh grass that we used to eat in The Garden" she remembered. The enjoyment of eating such deliciousness distracted her from the surroundings and any impending dangers that the outside world might bring. Further and further Savannah pushed into the clump until only her two perfectly tiny, pink, feet that only just touched the ground, were visible.

Without warning, something sharp clamped down hard on her foot, causing her to squeak out in pain. Quickly pulling her feet in behind her, she shot forward even further into the safety of the soft grass. The pain in her foot was a searing heat, which caused her to cry in pain. Fear gripped her mind, and her heart pounded like a drum.

"What happened? What was that? It hurts so much!" she wheeked. The outer edge of the grass began to shift; Savannah knew that whatever hurt her foot was on the move towards her now. "Maybe if I run fast enough and am quiet enough, I might find my way to the opening of the burrow, but then what?" she thought. "Or maybe the garden wall? I might find the opening and be able to return to the safety of The Garden!" Confusion had set in, but as Savannah was about to make her move, she could feel the ground begin to move slightly and was aware that the intruder was now quietly moving closer towards her. Gathering all her strength, she bravely leapt from the centre of the plant and to her amazement landed front feet first. No sooner had they hit the ground than she bounded another step, her legs shaking, and her whiskers twitching with fear. She could feel her enemy following closely behind her.

Filled with such fear, she dared not look back in case she should trip. The ground continued to rumble beneath her feet, causing her to dash to her right, bringing her close to the high brambled wall of The Garden. In an instant, the ground stopped shaking, and a loud hiss exploded behind her. "Run Savannah, run!" she screeched and shot to her left, heading back towards the safety of the burrow. Savannah knew that it was not safe being out in the open; she needed to reach the burrow as quickly as she could. Her chest was burning from the exertion, and she began to pant as she leapt into the burrow and landed on her side on the grassy nest she had made.

An imminent feeling of doom came over Savannah, she turned her body away from the opening, closed her eyes and lowered her head to the floor. Her heart felt as though it would explode at any moment. In her heart she cried out to the Great Gardener to help her, "Please let me live, I don't want to die!" She wheeked inside over and over. Instantly she felt the fear begin to subside but was once again forced back into the corner as a loud noise pierced the night, a screeching like no other, a creature in pain, and then silence.

Savannah couldn't move, she was so frightened, there was so much pain in her little body, and she could feel the sticky liquid coming from a hole in her foot. She kept her eyes closed, shaking in fear, she waited for the intruder to make his move. Instead, the beautiful voice of an angel called to her "Come on little one; I'm not going to hurt you! Come on!" A warm, soft hand slid underneath Savannah's exhausted body and lifted her, pulling her in close to the warmth and safety of her body. Savannah moved slightly, trembling and crying, she peered wide-eyed into the beautiful face of The Woman.

"The Woman! It's The Woman!" she squeaked at the top of her voice as though Lowey was nearby. Savannah could not stop wheeking with joy and moved up further to snuggle in under the Woman's neck.

Pulling her back down in front of her face, The Woman inspected Savannah, looking at her not with a smile but with her mouth pulled in tight. She took Savannah's little leg into her fingers and made a whooshing noise with her mouth and wiped away the sticky liquid with her finger, causing Savannah to grimace.

"We need to return this little one to her mate." The Woman spoke to the Man. Savannah moved her head a little between the enormous fingers and looked in the direction of The Man. He was standing next to the Woman holding in his hand what looked like a long tree branch. Savannah breathed in sharply when she realised that what he was holding was the Serpent. Its long shiny body was glistening in the moonlight, hanging so still. Its head had been crushed, and the tongue hung limply out of its mouth.

"You are a fortunate girl" The Man spoke looking directly at Savannah, "he only grabbed you with his fangs and didn't get them in all the way to cause you too much harm. What shall we do with this?" he said to the Woman, holding the Serpent up high. She looked down at her feet and smiled! The Man looked back at her and laughed the loudest laugh that Savannah had ever heard.

The Woman told the Man, "When we were coming along the top of the ridge I saw a couple of her kind running along and making a terrible racket; they came from that huge tree down in the clearing, she might belong with them."

Savannah began to wheek at the Woman. "Yes, I do I belong with them, that is my Lowey and our friends Constance and Avery. Can you take me there?"

"Oh, alright, enough now!" The Woman laughed. "We had better get her home before these little ones arrive in my hands!" she told the Man.

Savannah felt a wave of relief as they began to make the journey back, but instead of going along the wall of The Garden and back down the ridge, they walked down the ravine and towards another clearing in the opposite direction.

Savannah shrieked but was quickly silenced by the pain in her tummy again. Moments later, Savannah was placed into a soft bed of hay, surrounded by a wall of what looked like small tree trunks. It was a strange feeling of confusion and relief, as Savannah looked up, she could see the Man and the Woman sitting next to her. "Everything will be okay", the Woman cooed.

Exhausted, Savannah lay down in the nest made by the Man and the Woman and looked upon the two tiny creatures that had earlier given her so much pain - the memory of the experience now fading and replaced with feelings of such joy.

"Look what I created!" she wheeked up at the Man and the Woman, who had not left her side the entire time.

Two small bundles of curly damp fur snuggled in under Savannah's tummy; it was a strange feeling to have them tickling her on the outside giving her a sense of amazement, she could not take her eyes off them. Two perfect little boy pups had now been added to the family. The smaller of the two resembled Savannah. His fur was white, and ginger, with beautiful straight whiskers, and the other was a perfect replica of Lowey, a pure white nose, long black curly whiskers and a shock of brown and ginger hair on his head that stood up on end as it began to dry. Savannah continued to check over her pups and finished by counting their little digits, three on each foot and four on each of the paws, and a set of perfectly formed ears, "just like Lowey's," Savannah laughed to herself.

The joy of the new arrivals was suddenly interrupted as the basket was lifted gently from its resting place. The Man and The Women smiled down at Savannah as they began to walk out into the night air, the little ones shifted their position moving further underneath for protection.

Savannah was so tired and was relieved to be finally going home. Within, what felt like moments, she and the babies were lifted out of their warm bed and placed back into the hollow of the tree trunk. Constance was running around in circles, wheeking with joy that Savannah was home safely and was not alone.

"Oh, Savannah!" Constance cried. "Look what you and Lowey have created!"

CHAPTER 8

A Night Of Tales

T he evening had finally arrived, swirls of smoke twisted their way up into the air, the tiny white feathers twitched as Morton began to stir from his slumber. He wobbled his head from side to side and ruffled the majestic plumage on his body as he shook off the sleep. Leaning forward, Morton poked his head out of the hole in the tree and looked out over the clearing; it was a spectacular evening, just a slight breeze and clear skies, perfect weather for flying, one always needs to take stock of the weather before taking off. Looking down into the clearing he could see that the little band of friends had gathered in front of the warmth of a fire, Morton had no idea how a fire had started, but the smell was so comforting he didn't care about the finer details.

Hopping forward out onto the branch, he grasped the wood with his enormous clawed feet, stretched his wings out as far as they would go, let out a large hoot and stepped forward, keeping his wings outstretched he glided down and landed softly on the ground a short distance away from the group.

Avery was the first to spot him.

"Ah!! My dear chap come on over here and join us by the fire. We are having a splendid time. Savannah has been telling us her tale about how The Man and The Woman rescued her. Its riveting stuff, Old Thing!" Avery yelled. "Come, join us."

Morton was thrilled to be invited, he had heard about Avery and Constance from Lowey on their way home from the Ridge, and immediately recognised his strange way of talking. He couldn't help but have a little chuckle to himself, "Old Thing? What a cheek!" Morton began to walk towards the group, bouncing up and down, almost skipping as he went and finally settling next to Lowey. Constance and Savannah were looking at each other and wheeking out laughter that could not be controlled.

"What?" Morton said looking at the girls, his eyes seeming to pierce through them and the dark eyebrows above them pinched together into a frown. Constance coughed and wiped her eyes with the back of her paw and winced a little, the patch of fur that had been lost during the great Exodus still made her smart. Savannah gave her a quick nuzzle, "Oh, you're such a mum!" Constance laughed, which set them both off wheeking again.

"Avery, why don't you tell everyone what happened when we left the garden?" Constance suggested, finally pulling herself together and snuggling down next to Savannah. Constance enjoyed letting Avery take the lead, he was such a good storyteller and enjoyed putting on a show.

"Ok, but I am going to tell the tale as though I am reading to you, just for a bit of fun" he said and cleared his throat.

Avery had been enjoying the warmth of the morning sun, curled up fast asleep underneath some ferns that grew around the tree-lined edge of the garden. Each day in the garden was perfect and today was no different, a gentle breeze rolled over his silky fur as though caressing him. He reached out his front paws as far as they would go, giving his back a well-earned stretch and then he let out a contented yawn.

"Ah, this is the life old chap!" he thought to himself. Coming up onto all fours, he sat up and began to preen himself with his front paws, making sure to give his ears a good scratch in the process. It had been quite some time since he had eaten a good meal, at least two hours he thought, leaning towards Constance who was still sleeping.

Avery looked lovingly at Constance and nuzzled her with his nose. She was so tiny that when they slept, she just fit in underneath his armpit. Avery and Constance had been created for each other, just like all things in The Garden, he thought. He was so thankful to The Great Gardener for the gift of Constance; she was so much fun and understood him completely.

Avery sniffed at her ear and gave it a little nibble, "Come on old girl, it's time to wake up, I'm starving!" he rumbled.

Constance opened her eyes and blinked a couple of times, "Avery, is that your tummy I can hear rumbling?" She wheeked and let out a giggle.

"Well, yes, it is! Can't keep the tummy waiting, old thing!" He laughed. "Come on up you get," he said, looking back over his shoulder.

Constance jumped up and followed Avery, his legs were longer than hers, and she had to run part of the way to catch him up. They wandered a little way into the clearing. This part of the garden was incredibly beautiful; the grass was long and lush, and small white flowers were dotted everywhere, giving off the kind of scent that made you want to stop and smell them. On past the old fallen log and along the side of a vast patch of beautiful bushes laden with berries ready for the eating. Avery plucked a berry, tossed it in the air with his paw and opened his mouth as wide as he could, just snatching it out of the air with his beautiful white teeth. "Haha! he cried suddenly coughing and almost choking on the juice. He let some dribble down onto his fur and then wiped the rest from his lips and end of his nose with his paw.

"Did you see that old girl?" he called, "did you see how I caught that berry with my teeth?"

Constance laughed at him. "You're a clown, Avery!" she replied and tossed another berry into the air for him. Catching it in his teeth as he had done before, he wiggled over and gave it to Constance. "Here you are my lovely, this is for you" he said and blew her a kiss.

At some point during the feasting that followed, Constance looked up mid-mouthful and spotted the Man and the Woman hiding in some bushes nearby. Quickly finishing the berry, she quietly moved closer to the edge of the bush to get a clearer view. "Avery, come and see!" she called.

Avery looked up from where he was sitting and dropping his berry on the ground; he joined Constance. He couldn't help but notice that she had berry juice all over her face and quickly began to lick it away, "Can't let this go to waste, you know!" he wheeked, laughing. "So what's this all about, old girl?" he asked Constance.

"The Man and the Woman are hiding in those bushes, and the Great Gardener is looking for them!" she wheeked. "Why would they be hiding Avery?" Avery stopped preening Constance and looked to where the Man and the Woman had been, only to find that they were no longer there. He sat down and began to pull on his whiskers with his claws, pulling his eyes together into a frown. "I wonder where they could have gone?" he thought.

Moments later, Avery felt a strange vibration under his feet. "Do you feel that?" he asked Constance.

"Feel what?" she replied.

"There was a strange rumbling noise, and the ground began to vibrate, you didn't feel or hear that?" he asked. Constance was now sitting still and looking up at the sky, a strange noise was not just coming from the ground, but now the sky was rumbling too.

"Oh, Avery, what is that?" she squeaked worriedly.

"I just asked you the same thing, old girl!" he squeaked back. "Come on quickly Constance, try and keep up with me, we had better get under-cover." Without another word he set off running as fast as his legs would carry him. Constance did as she was instructed and stayed as close to Avery as possible but being so small, immediately found herself falling behind.

"Avery, wait!" Constance began to wheek, but the noise from the sky and the ground drowned her out. The sounds were growing louder, the sky was becoming darker, and what had been a delicious, delicate breeze in the air was quickly becoming a blustering wind. Constance ran faster, just managing to keep Avery in her sight. Suddenly Avery stopped and waited for her to catch up. Grabbing the fur on her side with his front teeth, he gently guided her along with him until they reached the safety of the ferns along the riverbank. Avery couldn't control his breathing, trying to catch his breath, he leaned into Constance to comfort her. "Are you alright, old girl?" he puffed.

"Oh, Avery, I'm scared, what is happening to our beautiful garden?" she cried out. The ferns were flapping above their heads as though they might fly away at any moment and were no longer able to provide them with the protection that they had sought. Leaves and dust filled the air as the ground continued to rumble. Constance pushed closer into Avery's large body and began to wheek at the top of her voice. Avery leaned into Constance and shouted into her ear, "Come on, it's going to be alright, I need you to be brave!" but almost immediately the floodgates opened up, and the sky emptied a deluge of water down onto the garden, and within moments what had once been a babbling brook that had lovingly supplied the residents of The Garden with great refreshment, became a terrifying raging torrent, ripping the riverbank into its clutches.

Avery was the first to hit the water and immediately sank below the surface, the cold water filling his nostrils and forcing its way down his throat. His little feet were paddling as fast as they could to bring him back up to the top. Within moments, he broke the surface coughing and squeaking at the same time. He was swept down the river at such a pace that he couldn't catch hold of anything to stop the ride, he tried to flip around and swim back upstream, but the raging waters kept pulling him further and further away from where they had fallen.

Occasionally, he managed to swim a little to the side, paddling as hard as he could with his feet, but he would then be pulled away again, his heart beating so fast that he thought the end was near. All he could think about was grabbing hold of something and trying to avoid the rocks. In front of him, the river began to slow a little, and there was a fallen tree, Avery swam as hard as he could off to the side and somehow managed to grab onto one of the branches. He pulled as hard as he could, his whole body shaking with the effort. Finally, he reached the sodden foliage near the bank and crawled up onto dry land once again. Looking around, he began to wheek for Constance, his cries becoming louder and louder, all the time hoping for a response.

Avery shook off as much water as he could and ran as near to the end of the fallen tree as he could manage without being dragged back into the water once again.

"Constance! Constance! Where are you, Constance?" he screeched, his wheeks becoming caught in his throat. The tears were coming so fast he could hardly see. He roughly wiped his eyes with the backs of his paws; he stood up high and began to call again.

"She has to be here!" he cried, and the next moment before he realised what he was doing, he had leapt back into the water and was swimming as fast as he could to the other side of the riverbank. He spotted her outline on the opposite side of the bank where the water must have swept her little body.

Dashing out of the water, he grabbed her wet fur on the back of her neck and pulled with all his might, dragging her onto the muddy bank. He pulled her as far away from the water as he could and began to push with his nose.

"Constance, are you alright, old girl? Speak to me!" he sobbed. She lay so still, her small lifeless body soaked from the water was so very quiet. Avery grabbed her by the scruff with his teeth again and pulled her as close as he could to himself. Looking up at the sky he called out to the Great Gardener, "How can you let this happen? We were all happy in the garden. We were not scared, and we were safe with you. Help us, please! I want to come home, please!" he cried out. Avery felt the devastation seeping deep into his bones and cried out again for the Great Gardener to help. Still looking up into the sky, Avery could see a patch where the dark cloud had receded, and sunshine shone through in stripes of magnificent bold colours. He had never seen anything quite so beautiful before and pulled Constance's limp body even closer.

"Look Constance isn't it beautiful?" he cried. "It's for you from The Great Gardner!" then without warning, her body twitched a little, then she began to cough, water started to come from her nose and mouth, and her eyes opened wide. Avery hugged her so tight he made her squeak.

"Constance, you're alive! You're alive, old girl!" he cried leaping to his feet. He wanted to run and jump and leap for joy, but he knew now was not the time for his usual antics.

Quickly settling himself, Avery sat down next to Constance who had managed to sit up and shake some water from her fur. He noticed that she had a large bump on the back on her ear. He leaned over and sniffed it, tickling her with his whiskers and making her giggle.

"Ouch," she said, looking at him, a smile started to form on her pouting lips and spread across her face. Avery looked at her and smiled. "I didn't even touch it."

"Oh, Avery, your tooth is missing!" Constance laughed, "oh, you do look funny."

Avery stuck a muddy digit into his mouth and fiddled with the three teeth that were left. He shook his head and grinned at Constance, "well if that's all the damage that's done, then I shan't be complaining!" he said, laughing. Snuggling into Avery's side, the pair lay in that small patch of coloured sunshine on the inlet of the riverbank in the mud until the exhaustion of the river had left them.

Time passed as Avery sat next to Constance and watched her sleep, he was not sure what had happened, but he knew deep down that The Great Gardener had opened the sky and given them a dry and warm, safe place to recover. Avery gently nudged Constance and placing his paw on her head he whispered to her to wake up.

"We had better find somewhere to stay before the night comes, we don't want to be out here in the open," Avery said. Constance slowly got to her feet, her fur was shaggy and muddied, she had a patch of fur missing from her leg, and her ear was a little torn. "She looks such a sight" Avery thought. Moving from one foot to the other, her teeth chattered a little, and the pain in her body from the ride down the river had set in. "Come on old girl, you can lean on me, I'll lead the way." As they stepped out of the patch of warm sun and headed up the embankment, the patch of sun moved with them. Avery had expected the wind and rain to hit them, but instead, it covered them and moved just a little ahead. It was a miracle, the patch of sunshine and colour were leading them; it led them right up to the trunk of a tree, which had an opening with piles of leaves and twigs scattered all around. As quickly as the patch of sun appeared, it vanished, leaving in its wake, a debris-filled blast of wind and pouring rain. Avery quickly shoved Constance from behind into the hole and followed, then immediately pushing the leaves and twigs into a pile, he covered the opening.

Constance noticed that there was a large nest on one side of the tree trunk which looked big enough for her and Avery to climb into for the night. After adding to the pile, they wiggled their weary bodies into the leaves and slept.

"The End." Avery smiled at his silent audience and took a bow.

Leaping to her feet, Constance wiggled over to Avery and gave him a gentle nuzzle, clapping her paws together. "Bravo Avery!!" She cried. Everyone else joined in, it had been a fantastic tale, and they had all survived the storm.

Lowey sat silently looking into the fire, the reflection from the flames lighting up his eyes, and as usual, he had a digit in his ear jiggling it around. "So, the sun led you to our tree trunk then?" he asked Avery

"Yes, old chap, that's it," Avery replied.

"After you cried out to the Great Gardener?" Lowey said, and Avery agreed.

Lowey pulled out the digit, looked at it and put it back into his ear. "Lowey!" Savannah laughed and pushed him with her foot, "don't you think Morton should tell his story now?"

"Sorry Morton, yes, quite right, Savannah it is his turn." Lowey said and gave his digit a little wiggle before removing it from his ear once again.

Now finally it was Morton's turn to speak, he looked around at the faces of each of the friends sitting around that fire, the flames eventually dying down. What had been blazing branches were now glowing red coals, small swirls of grey smoke broke off and drifted up into the night sky.

Cicadas could be heard scratching their legs together in the trees. Morton felt for the first time in days that he was safe and secure, he had found a new home with this strange but wonderful troop of friends. He finished thinking and looked up to find everyone waiting expectantly to hear his story.

It had been a day or two since the Exodus from the Garden. Morton had not had time to think about precisely what had happened, he knew only that in all the chaos he had lost his beautiful friend Genevieve. As he began to think about her, a lump started to form in his throat, and his eye began to well up with tears. Instantly he stood up tall on his feet and shook out his wings. How majestic he looked. So tall and regal. The feathers took on a life of their own, shimmering in the moonlight. This only made everyone even more curious about what Morton was about to say, causing them all to lean into the last remaining warmth of the fire. Morton sniffed, folded his wings back into place and sat back down, finally feeling that he was a little more in control of his emotions he cleared his throat with a small chirpy hoot.

Morton had liked the way that Avery had told his tale and decided that he would do the same.

Morton was jolted from his deep sleep by a rumbling sound, which was shaking the tree. Genevieve had begun to stir, sniffing the air and looking at Morton with bleary eyes, she nudged him with her beak.

"Morton, go and see what is going on outside! And what is that noise?" She grumbled. Genevieve was so warm and comfy in the nest, that all she wanted to do was go back to sleep. Surely, it wasn't night-time already, it felt like they had only just settled down to sleep.

The inside of the tree was warm and smelled like the moss that grew on the rocks of the stream on a warm summer's day. The darkness was a welcomed relief after a long day of foraging and nest making. Begrudgingly, Morton pulled himself up to the hole and cautiously peered over the edge and out into the clearing. Overhead, black clouds rolled and swirled angrily; the wind was blowing the branches of the trees, causing the leaves to fly off into the air. Morton wanted to pull his head back into the hole, but he was trying to make out what was happening to the ground below. He shook his head and rubbed his eye on his wing and looked out into the darkness, down below, he could see hundreds of creatures who lived in the garden, running in a huge pack.

"Gennie! Come and look at this, I have never seen anything like it! Quick!"

Genevieve poked her head out of the hole and was instantly hit in the face by a giant flying leaf. "Hoooo!" She shrieked and pulled her head back in. Morton turned around on his branch and looked back down the hole; Genevieve was sitting back in the nest with a look of surprise on her face. "I'm sorry Morton, I am not going back out there, even if it is night-time, we will get blown away!" she cried.

Morton scrambled back into the hole and sat in front of her on the nest. "It's going to be alright; you stay here, and I will go out and have a scout around."

With a look of relief on her face, she ruffled her feathers, puffing herself up and closed her enormous orange eyes. Morton sat for a while looking at Genevieve, wondering how she could sleep when outside the garden was turned upside down. With a disgruntled hoot, he returned to the branch, the sky was now completely black, and huge flashes of light could be seen in the sky. It felt as though something terrible was about to happen. In all their days in the garden, nothing like this had ever happened. Everyone had been so happy and content, and this feeling of dread that had come upon he and Genevieve was certainly nothing that they had encountered within the garden before. Morton began to shake a little, and he dug his huge claws into the branch to keep himself from being blown away, as another huge flash lit up the sky and was followed by an enormous crash.

Looking down at the ground below, Morton counted hundreds of creatures all moving together as one, the larger ones leading the way forward with some of the smaller animals scooting in and out between giant legs, only just escaping being trodden underfoot. The dust rose from the ground as the beautiful lush grass was crushed and torn. He suddenly spotted something shining and shimmering in the flashes of light; it was weaving in and out, slithering on its belly and occasionally rising.

"It's a Serpent," Morton thought, he had never seen one before, but for some reason, he knew exactly what it was, something that could not be trusted, a deceitful creature. Morton couldn't take his eyes off the serpent as it began to change direction, slithering between some rocks and disappearing into a grassy knoll. Another lightning flash lit up the sky and Morton could see the outline of a small rabbit sitting up on the knoll, its fur being blown wildly by the wind and drenched by the water that was pouring from the dark sky above. Fear gripped Morton inside; the little rabbit was lost and needed help.

Spreading out his wings, Morton pushed off the branch with a mighty heave, flapping his wings as hard as he could. He felt that there was no way that he would be able to glide down to the poor rabbit, the rain was stinging his eyes like needles. The wind was pushing him away from the direction of the grassy outcrop. The serpent had slithered its way around the rock and was now moving up behind the unsuspecting rabbit.

"Nooooo!" Morton hooted as he continued flapping his wings harder and harder. The rabbit was sitting up on its back feet and trying to wipe the rain from its eyes. Morton could see that it was only a baby and had probably become separated from its family. Screeching at the top of his lungs, Morton swooped down just in time to snatch the snake up in his clawed feet. The weight of the snake made it challenging to get some height, but he continued flapping as hard as he could. His heart was pounding so much his chest was burning with the effort. The snake was twisting and turning, trying to reach Morton's feet. A massive gust of wind swirled below, striking another blast and growing in such strength that the wind caught up under Morton's wings sucking him up higher until he felt the air becoming thinner. Looking down at the ground, he could see that he was no longer over the garden and that he was now outside. He could feel the snake still struggling, and without another thought, he opened his claws and dropped it. After losing the weight of the snake, Morton lost control in the strong wind and was blown downwards, landing in the top branches of a tree.

For a moment Morton was still. He was panting. His entire body shook from the effort that it had taken to stay up in the air. Feeling relieved that he had landed safely, he took a little more time to regain his composure and then leaping from the top of the tree with all his might, he mustered as much energy as he could in his exhausted wings and flapped his way back towards the garden.

Unexpectedly in front of him was a wall of brambles that had appeared out of nowhere. Redirecting his flight path, he flew straight up, flapping faster and faster, higher and higher. Morton could not believe that no matter how high he flew, he could not reach the top of the wall, it appeared to go on forever. The confusion was becoming overwhelming, and he cried out as he continued, small chirps of sadness were pouring out of his beak.

Defeated, he turned slowly and began to glide downwards, the air massaging his feathers as he floated down. Hot tears welled in his eyes and he shook his head, causing him to veer off course, and flew straight into the tree that he had left a moment before.

Morton screeched out in pain as he hit the top of the tree, tumbling through the branches and landing in the middle of the foliage.

He looked down at his leg, which was pinned between two branches. Grabbing hold of one branch with his beak to steady himself, he pulled his foot as hard as he could.

Morton began to struggle, flapping his wings to break free, but the pain in his foot shot up his leg, making his eyes water.

"Oh no, I must get out of here!" he hooted at the top of his voice. "I must go back to the garden to get Gennie!" he wailed. He struggled and flapped until he had no more strength left.

The rain continued to fall, although the sky was no longer alive with the dancing light show, and the rumbling was now off in the distance. Morton moved his body as close to the trunk of the tree as he could, trying to shelter his now drenched body. "I'm so thankful that Genevieve is safe in our tree." He sighed a little and shook off some more of the water. He thought about the little rabbit and hoped that it had found its family. He had always been fond of the little creatures in the garden and he especially had a soft spot for rabbits.

Morton looked up at Lowey and smiled, "and thankfully Lowey heard me and well, here I am."

Constance was sat upright staring at Morton and wiped away a secret little tear with the back of her paw.

"What happened to Genevieve?" she asked with a little quiver in her voice.

"I couldn't get back over the wall, but I know that she is safe up in our tree, and she knows that I will make my way back into the Garden eventually" he replied, nodding his huge brown head.

Lowey was laying back with a blade of dried grass wiggling about in his mouth, nibbling it down to the end as he listened to the last of the wood crackling, in an effort to stay alight. Suddenly Lowey was on his feet; he tossed the last of the hay from his mouth into the fire. He looked at all his friends with a small smile working its way up to his lips, he clasped his paws together, closed his eyes and nodded in such a way that made him look regal.

"My friends, tonight is a great night. It is the beginning of a beautiful fellowship between us. Let us stay forever together in this place; let it be called The Clearing, and we its people. Let the Great Gardener and the Spirit in the Garden be the ones who will lead and guide us. May we never leave their presence, for it is they who protect us and provide all that we need." Lowey took a deep breath in, and let it out slowly, he unclasped his paws and opened his eyes. Lowey felt an overwhelming sense that The Great Gardener and the Spirit in the Garden were with them. He looked at his friends once again; they all sat in silence, staring into the red embers of the fire and nodding their heads in agreement.

CHAPTER 9

The Way of the Covenant

Many seasons had come and gone since that night around the fire, a community had been born, and a way of life chosen. The world of The Garden though so close they could touch it, was out of reach, and sadly over the years many had tried to return but to no avail.

Lowey had grown in wisdom as well as years and consulted the Spirit in the Garden in all matters. He would not lean on his own understanding, but in all his ways he would follow the Spirit who would lead him.

It had been a beautiful summer's day and Lowey had spent most of it soaking up the sun on top of The Big Grey Rock not too far from the tree trunk. Stretching out his front legs as far as they would go, giving them a little bit of a shake, Lowey yawned the most giant yawn. His mouth opened wide, giving a birds-eye view of his enormous front teeth and the little pink glistening tongue. This rock had become the place where he spent most of his time lately, he could see the comings and goings of the folk in the little community. If he turned his head to the right, he could gaze up the hill to the perimeter of The Garden, and some days, if he was feeling energetic, he would take a slow waddle up the hill and sit close to the bramble wall and talk to the Spirit in The Garden.

Lowey found, in his later years, that many creatures in the community would come to talk with him. They would ask advice about many things, and even though Lowey was not the Knower of All Things, he took the responsibility very seriously and took great pride in finding out whatever they needed to know. He always ensured the information was given and that all of their needs were met. When he and Savannah had arrived in The Clearing, little did they know that they would become the ones that the new arrivals would look to for advice and that Lowey and Savannah would soon lead them in the right direction.

Today Lowey had decided that he would stay on his rock and sleep a little, he did have a great desire to climb the hill, but weariness was upon him and he had succumbed. His once large potato shape had flattened out over the years, giving him more of a pear-shaped appearance, and a little too much loose skin padded with the result of many feasts of berries and the like, was now spread out upon the smooth flat rock. The coolness from within the rock kept him comfortable as the morning sun warmed his back and shone on his once pristine fur, which had since become rather dull in colour and not as thick. The lush hair that had surrounded his face had long become wisps, giving him a very distinguished look. He had found it increasingly challenging to groom himself and relied more and more upon Savannah for his preening since he had lost the ability to reach around the sides of his body.

Scratching at his head with his paw, he inspected the nails; they too had become quite curled in his old age, certainly not the beautiful black pointed claws that once grabbed branches and plucked berries; the young ones helped him with foraging now. He smiled as he thought back to the days when he and Savannah had first encountered each other, how they enjoyed their time together, running and playing, foraging for food and of course the berry feasts, eating until they thought they would burst. Deep down in his heart, Lowey knew that his time in The Clearing was coming to an end. How he wished that they could have stayed forever in The Garden and not have to grow old and die.

Lowey closed his eyes and slept. He dreamed he was by the stream in The Garden again, the water bubbling along happily on its way to somewhere and dragonflies flying as close to the water as they dared without getting their feet wet. The light of the sun warmed his back as he gazed into the water. In his dream, he smiled at his reflection. "Lowey, you certainly were fearfully and wonderfully made." Lowey's reflection smiled back at him as the Spirit of The Garden wrapped its warm hug around him. Even in his dream he was so drained and just wanted to sleep, he lay down in the ferns that still grew along the banks of the stream, the little tendrils gently patting his head in the slight breeze that always ambled passed the river.

"Lowey, it's time," a voice called to him on the breeze. The Spirit in The Garden hugged him a little tighter, and Lowey shifted his body a little.

"Are you ready, Lowey?" the voice called again. "I am ready," Lowey thought.

"Well done good and faithful servant" The Great Gardener, called back.

Filled with such peace, Lowey felt all the little aches and pains that had been in his bones just float out of him, and his muscles relaxed in the warmth, he inhaled the sweet air only once more and then let it all go.

Lowey was acutely aware of a tickling feeling on his nose; little tendrils so very gently kissed his nostrils. He wriggled the end just enough to stop the tickling for a moment. Stretching out his front legs as far as they would go, he was acutely aware that the old familiar ache in his bones was no longer a bother. He stretched out even further. It felt so good he gingerly stretched out the back ones as well. The tickling commenced again, and he wafted away the annoyance with a wave of his paw. Opening his eyes, the colours in front of him were so vivid and the light so bright that he instantly clamped them shut again. This time squinting into the light, Lowey opened his eyes slowly, shadows of colour flowed around him rising and falling on the breeze.

Lowey opened his mouth to speak, but no words came. He lay there with the biggest pout on his lips, just staring up at the whirling colours. Off in the distance, all around him white billowing clouds blended in with the colours, their edges yellowing where they met.

Still lying on the ground, he realised that his Big Grey Rock was replaced with the softest of bedding, Lowey felt as he had done when he had first been created by the Great Gardener many years ago, only this was different. Lowey was alone, but he also felt a presence with him. Sitting upright, he was still astounded by the lack of pain in his body. He looked down at his paws, they were as they had been when he had first awoken in the garden; his ginger paws, with long black nails now restored to their former glory. Lowey was mesmerised.

"Focus, Lowey," he muttered to himself, "where am I?" he wondered. He could feel the tickling commence again, only this time it was in his tummy. Looking up into the sky he could see the bright colours going on forever; red, orange, yellow, green, blue, indigo and violet. He took one of his long black nails and popped it into his ear and wriggled it around, "Oh my, oh my ears!!" he cried.

Jumping to his feet, his body sprang into a life of his own, spinning and wiggling, front and back legs kicking out at the same time, he wheeked and wheeked at the top of his voice. The Spirit in The Garden twisted and twirled with him, creating a dance of such delight. There was a party! A party had begun at the end of the rainbow that day. The sky was filled with butterflies of all colours, shimmering and glistening; they formed pictures in the clouds as they danced and floated in unison on the breeze. After what seemed like an eternity, Lowey lay on his back in the softness looking up into the clouds. The butterflies began to form a funnel of colour which swirled closer and closer. The joy was flowing out of Lowey and filled every fibre of his being. As quickly as the butterflies gathered, they would separate creating a new vision. Lowey was mesmerised by the beauty of these creatures, not just their physical beauty but the gracefulness of their dance. One by one, the little creatures floated down and landed all around him, creating a cocoon, as their wings flapped the silver dust floated into the air and began to cover Lowey's magnificent coat. Filled with intense wonder, Lowey fell into such a state of peace, the butterflies started to slow and quieten down. Lowey could feel the Great Gardener nearby, his eyes immediately filled with such tears of love and joy.

"You're here! You're here, oh my, oh my heart," he cried out, weeping. The tears poured in torrents as he felt the words of the Great Gardener lay out in his soul.

"Lowey, you are my first creation of all the creatures that creep and crawl, from the earth I brought you and to the earth you returned. I am so proud of you Lowey, you did not leave me even though I forsook you. You led your people with wisdom, grace, mercy and love, and for this, you are my chosen one. I will make a covenant with you and all creatures, you will give an account of your lives, and I will walk with you on this, The Way of the Covenant until you return to the garden from where you came and stay in peace with me for all eternity."

Suddenly the butterflies' wings began to move, lifting them together, they swirled around Lowey in an exquisite dance, Lowey's soul soared with them. He was going home, back to The Garden and would live forever in peace, no tears, no pain and no suffering. He would walk with The Great Gardener and every living creature and hear their tale.

Lowey looked up at the butterflies, a smile of great contentment spreading across his perfectly pouty little lips, "Oh my, oh my Lord!" he sang.

Lowey stood up tall on his back legs and stretched up as high as he could, placing his beautifully restored paw over his eyes to block out some of the brightness from the rainbow. Far off in the distance he could see the entrance to The Garden. There it was, spread out before him in all its glory, just as he had remembered, but now the colours from the Way of the Covenant glorified its beauty.

Shaking his head, he placed a glistening, black claw into his ear and gave it a jiggle, then he smiled. "Oh my, oh my eyes! I can see The Garden!" Lowey cried.

Coming back down onto all fours he began to wiggle and leap about with joy, his shock of ginger fur catching the colours from the rainbow, almost hiding him from sight. Mid leap, a butterfly delicately floated down and landed on the tip of his nose, Lowey shook his head slightly, but the butterfly was not moving. Sitting down on his bottom, Lowey looked down his nose at the butterfly making him momentarily cross-eyed. The butterfly looked back at him, fluttering its wings and wafting some dust into his nose, causing a sneeze to catch there.

Lowey had seen many butterflies in his years but nothing like this one, it was of no particular colour but reflected the rainbow as it moved its wings. Its outline was an ink-black which was alive, moving in time with the colours. Each leg was long and sleek, giving it an elegance that was only to be experienced, and the antenna, long and curled. Lowey held out a paw to encourage it to leave his nose, as the sneeze that had been caught was now working its way down, causing Lowey to worry that the butterfly would be injured by the intensity of what was about to come. The sneeze finally erupted, causing Lowey to jump and the butterfly to ascend into the air just in time.

"Oh, I do apologise!" Lowey exclaimed as he shook his head and rubbed his nose with his little ginger paws. The butterfly continued to swirl and was suddenly joined by another, and then another. Before Lowey could stick a claw into his ear and wriggle it about, the air was filled with a swirling funnel of colour. Lowey sat mesmerised by the display, a scent of such delight filled the air, and finally, he realised that the Spirit of The Garden had returned.

Lowey was overjoyed by his arrival and immediately clasped his paws together in response, words began to pour into his heart, and a knowledge of what was happening was laid out in his mind.

Suddenly filled with such an incredible sense of anticipation, Lowey turned and stood up high, his little furry legs shook as though he would break into a dance at any moment. Finding it difficult to contain his joy, his heart pounded out an excited rhythm, and then, there she was, at the end of the rainbow, his Savannah. The anticipation that had been building inside him made Lowey explode into a run so fast that he felt like he was flying, wheeking at the top of his lungs, he cried out, "Savannah! Savannah! You're here, you've arrived!"

At the same time Savannah was running almost as fast as Lowey, and then finally they both took one last leap, they rolled together wheeking and purring. Lowey nuzzled her beautiful face, the ginger hair tickling his nose as it had always done, and her whiskers seemed longer than they had and sparkled in the sunlight.

"What has happened Lowey? Where are we?" Savannah cried. "Look at you Lowey; you are restored to when we first met in…" her words were suddenly cut off as she peered over Lowey to the end of the rainbow.

"Lowey, it's our Garden!" she squeaked. "All these years we have been trying to return, and now here it is! Can we go in? Have you been living in The Garden?"

Lowey shook his head. "I have only just arrived, Savannah, I was on the big grey rock, and I fell asleep. I dreamed I was back in The Garden, and the Great Gardener called to me, and when I awoke, I was here on The Way of the Covenant."

Savannah couldn't believe what she was hearing. "No, Lowey, you have been gone for three long years, I found you asleep on the Big Grey Rock on that awful day, and you wouldn't wake up, and now I've found you again."

Lowey could not stop looking at Savannah; she was as beautiful as the day she was created; she was perfect. They walked together as they always had, chatting about all that had happened, and taking in the majesty of The Way of the Covenant, each step bringing them closer to the entrance of The Garden which was no longer being guarded.

From behind, two perfectly round little bottoms could be seen happily wiggling their way along a rainbow of colour towards The Garden and following not too far behind, a funnel of swirling butterflies pirouetting and leaving behind in the air a trail of silver dust.

GENESIS 1-3
THE MESSAGE

Heaven and Earth

1 ¹⁻² First this: God created the
Heavens and Earth—all
you see, all you don't
see. Earth was a soup
of nothingness, a bot-
tomless emptiness, an
inky blackness. God's
Spirit brooded like a bird
above the watery abyss.

³⁻⁵ God spoke: "Light!"
And light appeared.
God saw that light was
good and separated
light from dark.
God named the light Day,
he named the dark Night.
It was evening, it was
morning— Day One.

⁶⁻⁸ God spoke: "Sky! In the
middle of the waters;
separate water from
water!" God made sky.
He separated the water
under sky from the
water above sky.
And there it was: he named
sky the Heavens;
It was evening, it was
morning— Day Two.

⁹⁻¹⁰ God spoke: "Separate!
Water-beneath-Heaven,
gather into one place;
Land, appear!"
And there it was.
God named the land Earth.
He named the pooled
water Ocean.
God saw that it was good.

¹¹⁻¹³ God spoke: "Earth, green up!
Grow all varieties of
seed-bearing plants, Every
sort of fruit-bearing tree."
And there it was.
Earth produced green
seed-bearing plants,
all varieties,
And fruit-bearing
trees of all sorts.
God saw that it was good.
It was evening, it was
morning— Day Three.

¹⁴⁻¹⁵ God spoke: "Lights!
Come out!
Shine in Heaven's sky!
Separate Day from Night.
Mark seasons and
days and years,
Lights in Heaven's sky to
give light to Earth."
And there it was.

¹⁶⁻¹⁹ God made two big
lights, the larger to
take charge of Day,
The smaller to be in
charge of Night; and
he made the stars.

God placed them in
the heavenly sky to
light up Earth
And oversee Day and Night,
to separate light and dark.
God saw that it was good.
It was evening, it was
morning— Day Four.

²⁰⁻²³ God spoke: "Swarm, Ocean,
with fish and all sea life!
Birds, fly through the
sky over Earth!"
God created the huge
whales, all the swarm
of life in the waters,
And every kind and spe-
cies of flying birds.
God saw that it was
good. God blessed
them: "Prosper!
Reproduce! Fill Ocean!
Birds, reproduce on Earth!"
It was evening, it was
morning— Day Five.

²⁴⁻²⁵ God spoke: "Earth, generate
life! Every sort and kind:
cattle and reptiles and
wild animals—all kinds."

And there it was: wild
   animals of every kind,
Cattle of all kinds, every
   sort of reptile and bug.
God saw that it was good.
26-28 God spoke: "Let us make
   human beings in our
   image, make them
   reflecting our nature
So they can be responsible
   for the fish in the sea, the
   birds in the air, the cattle,
And, yes, Earth itself, and
   every animal that moves
   on the face of Earth."
God created human beings;
   he created them godlike,
Reflecting God's nature.
He created them male
   and female.
God blessed them:
"Prosper! Reproduce!
   Fill Earth!
Take charge!
Be responsible for fish
   in the sea and birds in
   the air, for every living
   thing that moves on
   the face of Earth."

29-30 Then God said, "I've
   given you every
   sort of seed-bear-
   ing plant on Earth
And every kind of
   fruit-bearing tree, given
   them to you for food.
To all animals and all
   birds, everything that
   moves and breathes,
I give whatever grows out
   of the ground for food."
And there it was.
31 God looked over everything
   he had made; it was so
   good, so very good!
It was evening, it was
   morning— Day Six.

2 Heaven and Earth were
   finished, down to
   the last detail.
2-4 By the seventh day
   God had finished his work.
On the seventh day he rested
   from all his work. God
   blessed the seventh day.
He made it a Holy Day

Because on that day he rested
from his work, all the
creating God had done.
This is the story of how
it all started, of Heaven
and Earth when they
were created.

Adam and Eve

5-7 At the time GOD made
Earth and Heaven, before
any grasses or shrubs
had sprouted from the
ground— GOD hadn't
yet sent rain on Earth, nor
was there anyone around
to work the ground
(the whole Earth was
watered by underground
springs)—GOD formed
Man out of dirt from the
ground and blew into his
nostrils the breath of life.
The Man came alive—a
living soul!

8-9 Then GOD planted a garden
in Eden, in the east. He
put the Man he had just

made in it. GOD made all
kinds of trees grow from
the ground, trees beautiful
to look at and good to eat.
The Tree-of-Life was in the
middle of the garden, also
the Tree-of-Knowledge-
of-Good-and-Evil.

10-14 A river flows out of Eden
to water the garden and
from there divides into
four rivers. The first is
named Pishon; it flows
through Havilah where
there is gold. The gold
of this land is good. The
land is also known for a
sweet-scented resin and the
onyx stone. The second
river is named Gihon; it
flows through the land of
Cush. The third river is
named Hiddekel and flows
east of Assyria. The fourth
river is the Euphrates.

15 GOD took the Man
and set him down in
the Garden of Eden

to work the ground
and keep it in order.

¹⁶⁻¹⁷ GOD commanded the
Man, "You can eat from
any tree in the garden,
except from the Tree-of-
Knowledge-of-Good- and-
Evil. Don't eat from it.
The moment you eat from
that tree, you're dead."

¹⁸⁻²⁰ GOD said, "It's not good
for the Man to be alone;
I'll make him a helper, a
companion." So GOD
formed from the dirt of
the ground all the ani-
mals of the field and all
the birds of the air. He
brought them to the Man
to see what he would name
them. Whatever the Man
called each living crea-
ture, that was its name.
The Man named the
cattle, named the birds of
the air, named the wild
animals; but he didn't find
a suitable companion.

²¹⁻²² GOD put the Man into a
deep sleep. As he slept he
removed one of his ribs
and replaced it with flesh.
GOD then used the rib
that he had taken from the
Man to make Woman and
presented her to the Man.

²³⁻²⁵ The Man said, "Finally!
Bone of my bone,
flesh of my flesh!
Name her Woman for she
was made from Man."
Therefore a man leaves
his father and mother
and embraces his wife.
They become one flesh.
The two of them, the Man
and his Wife, were naked,
but they felt no shame.

3 The serpent was clever, more
clever than any wild ani-
mal GOD had made. He
spoke to the Woman: "Do
I understand that God
told you not to eat from
any tree in the garden?"

2-3 The Woman said to the
serpent, "Not at all. We
can eat from the trees
in the garden. It's only
about the tree in the
middle of the garden
that God said, 'Don't
eat from it; don't even
touch it or you'll die.'"

4-5 The serpent told the
Woman, "You won't
die. God knows that the
moment you eat from
that tree, you'll see what's
really going on. You'll be
just like God, knowing
everything, ranging all the
way from good to evil."

6 When the Woman saw that
the tree looked like good
eating and realized what
she would get out of it—
she'd know everything!—
she took and ate the fruit
and then gave some to
her husband, and he ate.

7 Immediately the two of
them did "see what's
really going on"—saw

themselves naked!
They sewed fig leaves
together as makeshift
clothes for themselves.

8 When they heard the sound
of GOD strolling in the
garden in the evening
breeze, the Man and his
Wife hid in the trees of the
garden, hid from GOD.

9 GOD called to the Man:
"Where are you?"

10 He said, "I heard you in
the garden and I was
afraid because I was
naked. And I hid."

11 GOD said, "Who told you
you were naked? Did you
eat from that tree I told
you not to eat from?"

12 The Man said, "The Woman
you gave me as a compan-
ion, she gave me fruit from
the tree, and, yes, I ate it."
GOD said to the Woman,
"What is this that
you've done?"

13 "The serpent seduced me,"
she said, "and I ate."

¹⁴⁻¹⁵ GOD told the serpent:
"Because you've done
  this, you're cursed,
  cursed beyond all cat-
  tle and wild animals,
Cursed to slink on your belly
  and eat dirt all your life.
I'm declaring war between
  you and the Woman,
  between your off-
  spring and hers.
He'll wound your head,
  you'll wound his heel."

¹⁶ He told the Woman:
"I'll multiply your pains in
  childbirth; you'll give birth
  to your babies in pain.
You'll want to please
  your husband, but he'll
  lord it over you."

¹⁷⁻¹⁹ He told the Man:
"Because you listened
  to your wife and ate
  from the tree
That I commanded you
  not to eat from, 'Don't
  eat from this tree,'

The very ground is cursed
  because of you; getting
  food from the ground
Will be as painful as having babies is for your
  wife; you'll be working in
  pain all your life long.
The ground will sprout
  thorns and weeds, you'll
  get your food the hard
  way, Planting and till-
  ing and harvesting,
  sweating in the fields
  from dawn to dusk,
Until you return to that
  ground yourself, dead and
  buried; you started out as
  dirt, you'll end up dirt."

²⁰ The Man, known as
  Adam, named his wife
  Eve because she was the
  mother of all the living.

²¹ GOD made leather cloth-
  ing for Adam and his
  wife and dressed them.

²² GOD said, "The Man
  has become like one of
  us, capable of knowing
  everything, ranging from

good to evil. What if he
now should reach out
and take fruit from the
Tree-of-Life and eat, and
live forever? Never—
this cannot happen!"

²³⁻²⁴ So GOD expelled them
from the Garden of Eden
and sent them to work
the ground, the same dirt
out of which they'd been
made. He threw them
out of the garden and
stationed angel- cherubim
and a revolving sword of
fire east of it, guarding the
path to the Tree- of-Life.

THE WAY OF THE COVENANT

Book 2

Genesis 9: 12-16 God continued, "This is the sign of the covenant I am making between me and you and everything living around you and everyone living after you. I'm putting my rainbow in the clouds, a sign of the covenant between me and the Earth. From now on, when I form a cloud over the Earth and the rainbow appears in the cloud, I'll remember my covenant between me and you and everything living, that never again will floodwaters destroy all life. When the rainbow appears in the cloud, I'll see it and remember the eternal covenant between God and everything living, every last living creature on Earth."17 And God said, "This is the sign of the covenant that I've set up between me and everything living on the Earth."

WRITTEN BY SUSAN TAYLOR-REEVES &
ILLUSTRATED BY LYNNE HUDSON
Inspired by the Word of God

INTRODUCTION

Time stood still in The Garden, Lowey and Savannah were once again reunited and would live in the peace that they had once known and loved. The Spirit in the Garden danced around them continually, placing His word into their hearts and minds, and The Great Gardener was no longer hidden behind the impenetrable wall.

When Lowey returned to The Way of The Covenant, The Great Gardener had named him His Chosen One, Lowey had been His first created Being that creeps on the earth, he was now privileged to greet and accompany all who came to The Garden, a position that Lowey had been created to hold and took very seriously.

The Garden was ever-expanding, continuously filling with creatures of all kinds, and Lowey had been very busy greeting each one at the end of The Way of the Covenant and walked with them to The Garden. Lowey would take each arrival on a journey back through their lives, listening to their tales and helping them to understand the plan that the Great Gardener had originally had for their lives and to now adjust to their new life in The Garden. Each creature brought with them magnificent tales as well as many questions that Lowey was only too happy to answer but always in consultation with The Great Gardener.

The Meadow was quite some way from the entrance to The Garden, and Lowey and Savannah had retreated there when she had first arrived. In the time since that awful day, The Great Gardener had been at work, creating a garden that was not to be compared with anything else in creation.

As they danced and skipped their way through the Garden, beyond the Woods, and out to the meadow, it was as though floating on air in a dream. They remembered how the Spirit in the Garden had wrapped Himself around them, giving a sense of love and peace, but this was something else, to be filled with an invisible glow, a feeling of contentment that only The Great Gardener could give. They were finally complete.

CHAPTER ONE
Part 1

The meadow lay before them in all its majesty, a carpet of yellow dandelions packed so tightly together, but somehow each one creating its own dance in the warmth of the gentle breeze. Savannah couldn't help but gasp with delight and wasted no time, running off headfirst into the yellow haze and disappearing. Lowey could hear her squealing and wheeking off in the distance, it took him back to the first day when they had met in The Garden, Savannah twirling and squeaking with joy at being created so beautifully by The Great Gardener. Lowey bounded headfirst into the flowers after Savannah and found her almost instantly laying on the soft carpet of green and munching on a dandelion. Lowey had quickly joined in, he lay down next to her and then plucking a lush green stem with his paw he popped the pointed end into his mouth, he nibbled it to the top with such ease, and then holding the flower in his paw he looked at Savannah with the cheekiest grin, his lips now green from the stem.

"Close your eyes and imagine that we are back in The Clearing," Lowey said to Savannah. "We are laying on the Big Grey Rock soaking up the sunshine together. Who is do you see?" Lowey asked.

"Constance, I really miss Constance" Savannah replied, "I wonder when she will arrive," she said opening her eyes and looking at Lowey.

"When the Great Gardener is ready to call her home to The Garden, she will appear at the end of The Way of the Covenant like we both did," Lowey said nodding at Savannah.

Gazing up, Lowey noticed that the stems of the flowers were such a bright green that they almost glowed, and the tiniest white fuzz coated them giving an appearance of softness which was comforting. The top of the stem met the head of the flower creating a hand that gently held it in place, and the golden colour of the dandelion almost gave off a light of its own.

Lowey and Savannah lay mesmerised by the glory of The Great Gardeners work until a butterfly floated down through a hole in the canopy of flowers and landed on Lowey's nose. Savannah began to giggle and tried to waft at it with her paw, but as she wafted at the creature her paw ran through it as though it were not even there. Savannah sat still, her beautiful red eyes blinking in awe at the butterfly. Its colours changing with each movement picking up the gold and green of the meadow and sprinkling silver dust over Lowey's face.

Lowey sat up and shook himself off wafting the dust into the air, he smiled at Savannah and began to wiggle his way after the butterfly. Savannah knew that Lowey was going to The Way of the Covenant to greet a new arrival, she sat watching him wiggle his perfectly round bottom into the distance and disappear into the colours of the rainbow.

The peace that originally filled the Garden gave Savannah a little hug, reminding her that she was back where she belonged, and with a twist and a leap in the air she happily trotted back the way she had walked with Lowey, and into the cool of the Woods which was filled with the most tantalising smells of berries and fruit.

The Garden was in full bloom and Savannah moved with a slow wiggle in and out of the flowers, stopping and sniffing each one, drinking in the dreamy and delicious fragrance that filled the air. Continuing her way through the Woods she couldn't help but wonder who Lowey had gone to meet at the end of The Way of the Covenant, secretly hoping it was Constance.

Savannah suddenly she found herself at the base of an enormous oak tree bringing her to an abrupt stop.

"Oh dear, I had better look where I am going" she giggled to herself looking up into the tree.

The trunk appeared to go on forever, Savannah could not remember ever seeing a tree of such size, there appeared to be no end, it just continued up and blended into the colours of the sky, in greens, golds, and blues. She began to walk around the enormous base of the tree, but also found that no matter how far she walked it did not bring her back to where she had started. She lay down on the ground and peered up into the branches, the foliage wrapped itself around the branches giving it a softness that appeared to be the lining of everything in this new garden. Far up in the tree Savannah could see there was a white shape nestled in the branches, squeezing her eyes into a squint to get a better look at the outline it was obvious that this was no ordinary creature.

"It's an Owl!" she heard Lowey say in her head, which made her laugh out loud.

For the longest time, Savannah lay at the base of the tree staring up into the canopy at what looked like an owl, but there was something a little strange about the markings and the sheer size of the creature, it certainly did not look like an everyday owl.

Leaping to her feet Savannah thought perhaps she could get the owl's attention by rumbling around the base of the tree, it was a fun thing to do even if the owl didn't notice. Savannah took off wiggling her bottom from side to side and purring as loudly as she could, throwing in a leap and a kick for good measure here and there.

Suddenly Lowey was at her side and joined in, which completely put Savannah off. "Lowey!" she squeaked and pushed him with her foot.

Lowey just fell about squeaking with laughter, and Savannah couldn't help but laugh as well. "What were you doing?" Lowey asked

"Look up in the tree Lowey, it's, an owl I think?" Savannah questioned. Lowey was silent, he was looking high up in the tree. "Well, it does look sort of like an owl," he said straining to see more clearly. Lowey stood up on his back feet and began to wave his paws franticly at the creature and began to wheek at the top of his voice. Without any warning, the giant creature leaped from the branch spreading out its enormous wings and glided majestically down towards Savannah and Lowey who quickly moved out of the way.

The pair stood transfixed, the creature that had flown down to them had the form of an owl but looked totally different, instead of two wings there were six. She stood so tall that Lowey and Savannah could only see her legs, they were a glistening silver with clusters of jewels, and the claws on each silver toe sparkled and changed with the colours in the sky. She suddenly began to descend from where she was standing pulling her legs up under her feathered body and sprinkling the air with silver dust as she sat down.

A glorious smell, sweet, floral, and powdery filled their nostrils as she fluffed the feathers on her body, almost as a bird would as it settled on the water after landing. Lowey looked at Savannah with a goofy look on his face, he was grinning from ear to ear.

"Savannah can you smell that?" Lowey asked. Savannah just nodded and looked back at the creature with a satisfied sigh.

The owl's body was a brilliant white, it was so bright that everything around her shone, and on the front and back of her wings, each feather was adorned with a huge eye, each one a different colour.

Savannah was certain that the eyes on the feathers were watching her but quickly dismissed the nonsensical though.

"A peacock has feather eyes" she whispered to Lowey, "Do you think they are feather eyes? I think they are!" she rattled on. Lowey just ignored her and continued to stare at the magical beast in front of him.

"Oh my, oh my ears, how rude!" he blurted out. "Introductions! My name is Lowey, and this is my Savannah, and I am the Greeter at the entrance to the Way of The Covenant" he announced with a smile.

The owl opened its large black beak and a piercing screech so loud came out that Lowey and Savannah were blown backward.

'Oh, my ears! Oh, your ears! Are you alright' he squeaked at Savannah who was rolling from her back onto her feet, 'Uh-huh!' she replied.

The owl began to move its huge white feathered head down close to Lowey and Savannah and whispered,

"I am so sorry! It has been some time since I have spoken out loud. The Great Gardener and I don't need to use our voices, well not for talking, and you are the first who have returned to the Garden that I have wanted to meet."

"My name is Genevieve, and I am one of The Great Gardeners recreations" she hooted in a soft melodic voice.

"The few of us who were left behind have been recreated so that we could stay forever with The Great Gardener." Each word that she spoke was as though it was sung, and Lowey and Savannah were once again left in a state of awe, with little hearts pounding with joy.

Lowey looked up into the bluest eyes that he had ever seen, the enormous black pupils surrounded by the deepest pools of blue appeared to go on forever like the tree, no end in sight. He instantly knew that this was Morton's Gennie, Morton had never stopped searching for her, it had become his lifetimes work to find her, and even up until Lowey returned home to the Garden she was still lost to him, well she wasn't lost it appeared she had never left The Garden.

"Oh, Genevieve, I am so pleased to make your acquaintance finally, Morton told us all about you and what happened on that awful and sad day." Lowey said.

The great creature looked at Lowey and happiness filled her eyes, large tears forming in the base of the blue.

"Oh, Morton, how I loved him, I am awaiting his return still" she sang in her beautiful angelic voice. "Perhaps when he returns you can lead him here to me. Though I am sure he will not miss me?" she hooted with a laugh.

"What happened Gennie? Why didn't you leave the Garden and find Morton? He never stopped looking for you, and well, he was so sad that he wasn't able to return to help you." Savannah squeaked up at the owl.

"One question at a time Savannah" Lowey wheeked back at her, giving her a nudge with his nose.

Genevieve sat looking at Lowey and Savannah, her beautiful blue eyes swirling around the enormous black pupils, she ruffled her feathers, wafting the sweet scent into the air once again. Lowey could see that she was searching for a way to tell them what had happened, it clearly was not going to be a story that would be like any other.

"Well" she began. "Morton told me to stay in our nest, he went out to see what was happening, I fell into a deep sleep, and didn't wake up. The Great Gardener found me on the ground outside of the tree, He breathed life into me and when I woke up, I was a new creation, a recreated being, and here in the new Garden." She shifted her huge body again as if trying to find a comfortable position to sit and looking down at her eager audience she continued.

"The Great Gardener said that no creature was able to live on in the Garden after what had happened, only four of us remained. Even if Morton had somehow been able to return to The Garden he would not have found me. The Great Gardener could no longer walk with His creations on Earth, so we returned to the New Garden by The Way of the Covenant."

Lowey looked over at Savannah, and ever so gently gave his ear a little wiggle with his paw, "but we could talk to The Great Gardener, and the Spirit in the Garden, they were still there I'm sure, I spent many long hours with them, we never left the Garden wall and they never left us!"

"Lowey is telling the truth" Savannah assured Genevieve. "I was the same, and many of the others in The Clearing, we promised to always stay close to the wall."

Genevieve smiled and nodded, her face suddenly softening, even more, causing Lowey to stand up on his back legs for a closer look. One of her wings lovingly wrapped around Lowey and lifted him into the air in front of her face, with the other wing she lifted Savannah. Forming a warm bed of feathers in front of her she began to sing to them, it was a voice like no other, the words coming from her beak were unfamiliar to both Lowey and Savannah, but immediately they understood in their hearts and minds that the Great Gardener was everywhere not just near the Wall and in The Garden. He wasn't hiding from them behind the wall, it was just a place that had connected them once, it was a place that they felt safe. The Great Gardener was with them everywhere they went.

Genevieve finished singing and gently lowered them to the ground, "so now you understand Lowey and Savannah, you carried them with you in your heart, your mind, and soul."

Genevieve had finished telling her incredible tale to Lowey and Savannah and as quickly as she had appeared, she returned once again to the branches of the massive tree and blended back into the foliage, and way up in the distance they could hear her singing "Holy, Holy, Holy".

www.ingramcontent.com/pod-product-compliance
Lightning Source LLC
LaVergne TN
LVHW021403080426
835508LV00020B/2430

Return
to the
Garden

INSPIRED BY THE CREATION STORY – GENESIS

WRITTEN BY *Susan Taylor-Reeves*

ILLUSTRATED BY Lynne Hudson

Ark House Press
PO Box 1722, Port Orchard, WA 98366 USA
PO Box 1321, Mona Vale NSW 1660 Australia
PO Box 318 334, West Harbour, Auckland 0661 New Zealand
arkhousepress.com

Cataloguing in Publication Data:
ISBN: 978-0-6450153-2-4 (pbk)

Design by initiateagency.com